Deck & Landscape Construction

Complete Handyman's Library™
Handyman Club of America
Minneapolis, Minnesota

Published in 1995 by
Handyman Club of America
12301 Whitewater Drive
Minnetonka, Minnesota 55343

Published by arrangement with Cowles Creative Publishing, Inc.
ISBN 0-86573-747-9

Printed on American paper by
R. R. Donnelley & Sons Co.
00 99 98   / 5 4 3 2

CREDITS:
Created by: The Editors of Cowles Creative Publishing
and the staff of the Handyman Club of America
in cooperation with Black & Decker. **BLACK&DECKER**
is a trademark of Black & Decker (US), Incorporated
and is used under license.

Handyman Club of America:
   Book Marketing Director: Cal Franklin
   Book Marketing Coordinator: Jay McNaughton

Contents

Introduction

Building landscape construction projects and adding a deck are some of the most basic and satisfying home improvements you can make. You will enjoy and use the outside of your home more, and be delighted with how attractive your home is. The instructions and step-by-step photography in *Deck & Landscape Construction* show you how to make these improvements and guide you every step of the way.

The first half of the book provides you with all the information you need to build exciting landscape projects. In the first section, on landscape planning, all the materials used in constructing these projects are shown, from timbers and precast concrete blocks for retaining walls to wood chips, rock, brick or flagstone for walkways and patios. You see how to pick the best material for the exact look and function in your landscape. Plus you learn how to choose the right tools to do the work.

Then, in the landscape construction section, you find out how to design and build your landscape project. All the techniques for constructing a retaining wall, a free-standing wall, walkways and paths, garden steps, a patio, a wood fence or a garden pond are presented. Every tool tip and construction method you need to produce quality work is shown.

The second half of the book is a comprehensive deck building manual. The first section, on planning, contains everything you need to know about the lumber, hardware, fasteners and concrete you need to build your deck. Then you see how to design your deck to meet local building codes, draw the necessary plans and order the lumber and materials.

The next section contains how-to instructions for the basic deck building techniques that will enable you to construct a deck of any design. Installing a ledger; locating, digging and pouring footings; setting posts; installing beams and joists; laying decking; building stairs and railings and applying a finish—all the essentials are demonstrated so that you can build a professional-quality deck.

Finally, two basic deck building start-to-finish sequences show how the steps in a project actually occur. These sequences will help you in planning and executing your own project.

Deck & Landscape Construction provides all the information you need to build exceptional projects for your home. The simple, easy-to-follow instructions will help make your work safe and successful. And these exciting and beautiful additions to your house and landscape will help you enjoy your home more than ever.

Plan ahead and be patient when designing your new landscape projects. Remember that plants grow and spread, and stone and wood structures change appearance as they weather. Landscape designers say that it takes at least five years for a landscape to reach its finished look. In the terraced retaining walls shown above (inset), the owner chose to plant a few well-spaced shrubs and perennials. Several years later (larger photo), this attractive yard is approaching maturity without being overcrowded.

Landscape Planning

Any landscape project you want to build should be planned so that it fits into your overall landscape design plan. The size and shape of a project should match the intended plantings and the place it will occupy in the landscape, as well as blend in with other landscape features. The materials used should relate to the colors, textures, and materials of your house, yard, and other landscape structures.

A detailed landscape plan takes time to develop, but helps ensure smooth work and successful results. Your finished plans should include detailed drawings, an accurate budget, a list of materials and tools, and a realistic time schedule.

Evaluate your existing landscape carefully as you begin to plan. To save money and time, plan the new landscape so it makes use of existing features that are both attractive and functional— a favorite flower garden, a garden walk, or a healthy tree, for example. You can transplant many hardy bushes and most perennial flowers from one part of your yard to another to fit a new landscape plan.

Although most of the projects shown in this book can be done without a work permit, always check with the local inspections office before you begin. If a building permit is required, you will need to have the inspector check your work.

Tips for Landscape Planning

Obey local "setback" regulations when planning fences, walls, and other landscape structures. The setback distance, determined by the local Building Code, prevents you from building any structure too close to property lines. Call your community inspections office to learn about any other restrictions on how and where you can build landscape structures.

Talk to your neighbors about your landscaping plans. Many projects, like building a fence, or planting a large shade tree or hedge, will affect neighbors as well as yourself. Keep the peace and avoid legal disputes by making sure your neighbors do not object to your plans.

Locate buried utility lines. Public utilities, like power, telephone, gas, and water companies, are required by law to inspect your site on request and mark locations of all buried lines. If your project requires digging or excavation, make sure your work will not interfere with underground utility lines.

Measure your yard, including the locations of all permanent landscape features. Accurate yard measurements are essential for drawing plans and estimating the quantities and costs of materials.

Interlocking block (below) is made from molded concrete that is split to provide a rough face resembling natural stone. Available in several colors and sizes, interlocking block is used for both straight and curved retaining walls, terraces, and raised planting beds. Interlocking-block walls create bold geometric patterns.

Concrete block is available in plain or decorative types. This durable building material is used often for free-standing garden walls. The hard, plain look of a concrete block wall can be softened with climbing plants or a surface application of stucco or stone veneer.

Poured concrete is durable and less expensive than other paving products. Although concrete is plain in appearance, it is easy to maintain, making it a popular choice for walkways, patios, walls, and steps.

Landscaping Materials

Stone, masonry, and wood are primary building materials for landscape construction. Stone and masonry give your landscape structures a feeling of permanence. Wood has a natural, warm look, is easy to shape, and can be painted or stained to match existing structures.

Whenever possible, choose landscape materials that either match or complement the materials already used on your home. For example, if you have a brick home, a patio made from similar brick will be more appealing than a poured concrete slab. Or, if you have a Tudor-style house

with exposed beams, a retaining wall built from rough timbers is more appropriate than a wall built from interlocking concrete blocks.

Man-made stone products cast from concrete are a good choice for landscape structures, considering the increasing price and dwindling supplies of forest timber and natural stone. Interlocking concrete block, brick pavers, and other manufactured stone products are widely available, easy to install, and very durable.

If you prefer the look of natural stone, try to select a type of rock that is common in your geographic region. Local stone makes your landscape look natural, and it is much less expensive than stone that must be shipped long distances.

Interlocking pavers
made from molded concrete are used in patios, walkways, and driveways. Available in a variety of colors and shapes, interlocking pavers are a good way to add distinctive patterns to a landscape.

Brick is an elegant, traditional building material made from molded, oven-dried clay. Available in many styles, brick is used to build patios, walkways, edging, and free-standing garden walls.

Terra cotta and adobe are molded clay products that are dried in the sun. They are used for patios, walkways, and garden walls. These products have a porous surface that can be damaged by water, so terra cotta and adobe are best suited for very dry climates.

Concrete pavers are made from poured concrete, and are available in many decorative shapes, textures, and colors. Inexpensive and easy to install, concrete pavers are used for patios, walkways, and steps.

9

Crushed
gravel

Smooth
river
gravel

Natural Stone

Gravel comes in
two forms: rough gravel
made by crushing larger
rocks, and smooth gravel
usually dredged from rivers.
Gravel is sorted by size, and has
many landscape uses. Applied as a
loose layer, gravel makes an informal, easy-
to-maintain pathway. Laid in large beds,
gravel lends a relaxed feeling to a landscape while providing texture and color.

Cut stone
(granite)

Cut stone, sometimes call ashlar, is natural
stone that has been cut into cubic shapes.
Marble, hard limestone, and granite (shown
here) are popular for cut stone. Cut stone is used
for both mortared or unmortared walls, patios or
walkways. It is an expensive, top-quality building
material that gives landscape structures an
elegant, timeless appearance.

Flagstone

Flagstone is uncut sedimentary stone that has naturally flat surfaces. Limestone, slate, and shale are common types of flagstone. Flagstone works well with
large, expansive landscapes, and is used for walkways, patios, and steps. It is a durable, but expensive,
paving material.

Rubble stone is any type of irregular, uncut
rock collected from fields, gullies, or stream
beds. It can include boulders, glacial debris,
rough pieces of quartz or granite, random
pieces of limestone or sandstone, or
even volcanic rock. Rubble stone often
is used in garden walls and retaining walls, and works best in informal, rustic landscapes. Rubble
stone is cheaper than cut stone.

Accent rock is distinctive
natural stone used as decora-
tion rather than as a building
material. Large, colorful rocks
can be partially buried in a
planting area or lawn to add
visual interest. Accent
rocks can range in size
from small 20-lb.
pieces to enormous
boulders weighing
more than a ton.

Glacial
rubble stone

Accent rock
(quartz blend)

Wood

Wood and bark chips are used for loose-fill on soft pathways or as a ground cover for planting areas. Wood and bark chips are inexpensive and lend a relaxed, casual look to a landscape.

Pressure-treated pine contains pesticides and wood preservatives to make it last. Less expensive than cedar and redwood, pressure-treated pine is used to build fences, retaining walls, raised planting beds, and garden steps. Most pressure-treated pine is green when new, but gradually weathers to a neutral gray. Or, it can be stained to resemble redwood or cedar. In some areas, treated pine also is available in a dark-brown color.

Cedar is a soft wood with a rough texture. It has natural resistance to decay and insect damage, and is used for fences, trellises, and arbors. Use cedar in above-ground structures only: where wood will be in contact with the ground, use pressure-treated lumber instead.

Redwood is a smooth-grained wood with a natural resistance to insects and decay. It is used for above-ground structures, like fences, trellises, and overhead arbors. Avoid using redwood where a structure will be in contact with the ground: for these applications, use pressure-treated wood instead. Because of high demand and dwindling supplies, redwood is becoming more expensive.

Redwood bark chips

Pressure-treated pine

Wood chips

Cedar

Redwood

Estimating & Ordering Materials

Use this chart to help you estimate the materials you will need for landscaping projects. Sizes and weights of materials may vary, so consult your supplier for more detailed information on estimating materials.

If you are unfamiliar with the gravel and stone products available in your area, visit a sand-and-gravel supplier to see the products first-hand.

When sand, gravel, and other bulk materials are delivered, place them on a tarp to protect your yard. Make sure the tarp is as close to the work area as possible.

Methods for Estimating Materials

Sand, gravel, topsoil (2" layer)	surface area (sq. ft.) ÷ 100 = tons needed
Standard brick pavers (4" × 8")	surface area (sq. ft.) × 5 = number of pavers needed
Poured concrete (4" layer)	surface area (sq. ft.) × .012 = cubic yards needed
Flagstone	surface area (sq. ft.) ÷ 100 = tons of stone needed
Interlocking block (6" × 16" face)	area of wall face (sq. ft.) × 1.5 = number of stones needed
Retaining wall timbers (5" × 6" × 8 ft.)	area of wall face (sq. ft.) ÷ 3 = number of timbers needed
Cut stone for 1-ft.-thick walls	area of wall face (sq. ft.) ÷ 15 = tons of stone needed
Rubble stone for 1-ft.-thick walls	area of wall face (sq. ft.) ÷ 35 = tons of stone needed
8 × 8 × 16 concrete block for free-standing walls	height of wall (ft.) × length of wall × 1.125 = number of blocks

Tools for Landscape Construction

Most landscape construction projects can be done with ordinary garden tools and workshop tools you already own. If you need to buy new tools, always invest in high-quality products. A few specialty tools, most of which can be borrowed or rented, make some jobs easier.

When using power tools outdoors, always use a GFCI (ground-fault circuit-interrupter) extension cord for safety. After each use, clean and dry metal tools to prevent rust.

A sturdy wheelbarrow is an essential tool for landscape construction and maintenance. Better wheelbarrows have inflatable rubber tires and wooden handles.

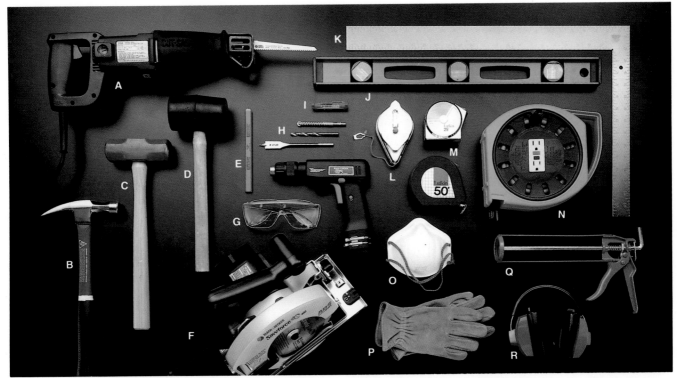

Basic hand and power tools used in landscape construction include: (A) reciprocating saw, (B) hammer, (C) hand maul, (D) rubber mallet, (E) pencil, (F) circular saw, (G) eye protection, (H) drill with bits, (I) line level, (J) carpenter's level, (K) carpenter's square, (L) plumb bob and chalk line, (M) tape measures, (N) GFCI extension cord, (O) particle mask, (P) work gloves, (Q) caulk gun, (R) hearing protectors.

Specialty tools you can rent include: (A) tamping machine, (B) "jumping jack" tamping machine, (C) sod cutter, (D) power auger, (E) hand tamper, (F) chain saw.

Tools for masonry work include: (A) mortar bag, (B) masonry chisel, (C) V-shaped mortar tool, (D) stiff broom, (E) masonry drill bits, (F) concrete float, (G) pointed trowel, (H) standard trowel, (I) rubber gloves, (J) masonry saw blade.

13

Common supplies for landscape construction include: (A) sheet plastic, (B) landscape fabric, (C) burlap, (D) stucco lath, (E) bendable rigid plastic edging, (F) post caps, (G) wood sealer-preservative, (H) mason's string, (I) rigid plastic edging, (J) flexible plastic edging, (K) rope, (L) perforated drain pipe, (M) masonry sealer, (N) splash block for runoff water.

Landscaping Supplies

In addition to the visible design materials used in a landscape (pages 8 to 11), there are many hidden, structural supplies that are equally important to successful landscaping projects.

Because landscape structures are exposed to weather extremes, make sure to invest in the best materials you can afford. Buying cheap materials to save a few dollars can shorten the life span of a landscape structure by many years.

Metal connecting materials, including nails, screws, fence hardware, and post anchors should be made from aluminum or galvanized steel, which will not rust.

Check grade stamps on pressure-treated lumber. Look for lumber treated with chromated copper arsenate, identified by the "CCA" label printed on the grade stamp. For above-ground and ground-contact applications, choose lumber graded "LP-22" or ".40 retention." If wood will be buried, use lumber graded "FDN" or ".60 retention," if it is available.

Base materials for landscape walls and paved surfaces include: (A) sand, (B) seed gravel, (C) compactible gravel subbase containing a large amount of clay and lime, (D) topsoil, (E) coarse gravel, used as backfill, (F) mortar mix, and (G) concrete mix.

Connecting materials for landscape construction include: (A) galvanized common nails, (B) galvanized finish nails, (C) self-tapping masonry anchors, (D) galvanized utility screws, (E) 12" galvanized spikes, (F) concrete reinforcement bars, (G) lead masonry anchors, (H) metal pipes for anchoring timbers, (I) lag screws with washers, (J) construction adhesive, (K) J-bolts, (L) galvanized post anchor, (M) rafter strap, (N) fence bracket.

Terraced retaining walls work well on steep hillsides. Two or more short retaining walls are easier to install and more stable than a single, tall retaining wall. Construct the terraces so each wall is no higher than 3 ft.

Building a Retaining Wall

The main reason to build retaining walls is to create level planting areas or prevent erosion on hillsides. But if you have a flat yard, you also can build low retaining wall structures to make decorative raised planting beds and add visual interest to the landscape.

No matter what material is used, a retaining wall can be damaged if water saturates the soil behind it. To ensure its durability, make sure your wall contains the proper drainage features (page opposite).

Retaining walls taller than 3 ft. are subject to thousands of pounds of pressure from the weight of the soil and water, so they require special building techniques that are best left to a professional. If you have a tall hillside, it is best to terrace the hill with several short walls (photo, above).

Before excavating for a retaining wall, **check with local utility companies** to make sure there are no underground pipes or cables running through the site.

Everything You Need for Retaining Walls:

Tools: wheelbarrow, shovel, garden rake, line level, hand tamper, rented tamping machine, small maul, masonry chisel, eye protection, hearing protectors, work gloves, circular saw, level, tape measure, marking pencil.

Materials: stakes, mason's string, landscape fabric, compactible gravel subbase, perforated drain pipe, coarse backfill gravel.

Added supplies for interlocking block walls: masonry blade for circular saw, caulk gun, construction adhesive.

Added supplies for stone walls: masonry chisel, masonry blade for circular saw, trowel, mortar mix.

Added supplies for timber walls: chain saw or reciprocating saw, drill and 1" spade bit, 12" galvanized spikes.

Options for Positioning a Retaining Wall

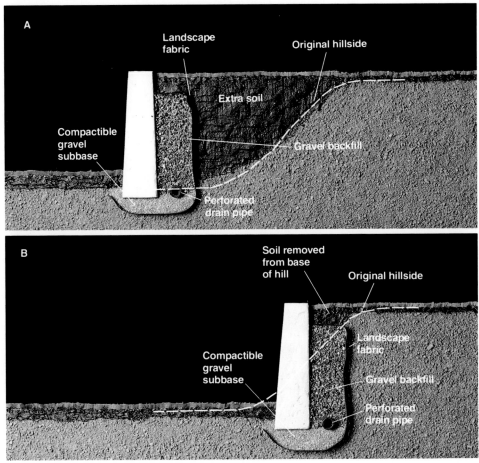

(A) Increase the level area above the wall by positioning the wall well forward from the top of the hill. Fill in behind the wall with extra soil, available from sand-and-gravel companies.

(B) Keep the basic shape of your yard by positioning the wall near the top of the hillside. Use the soil removed at the base of the hill to fill in near the top of the wall.

Structural features for all retaining walls include: a compactible gravel subbase to make a solid footing for the wall, coarse gravel backfill and a perforated drain pipe to improve drainage behind the wall, and landscape fabric to keep the loose soil from washing into the gravel backfill.

Providing Drainage for Retaining Walls

Backfill with gravel and install a perforated drain pipe near the bottom of the gravel backfill. Vent the pipe to the side or bottom of the retaining wall, where runoff water can flow away from the hillside without causing erosion.

Dig a swale, a shallow ditch 1 ft. to 2 ft. away from the top of the wall, to direct runoff water away from the retaining wall. This technique is useful for sites that have very dense soil that does not drain well.

How to Prepare a Retaining Wall Site

1 Excavate the hillside, if necessary, to create a level base for the retaining wall. For interlocking blocks or stone walls, allow at least 12" of space for gravel backfill between the back of the wall and the hillside. For timber walls, allow at least 3 ft. of space. When excavating large areas, rent earth-moving equipment or hire a contractor.

2 Use stakes to mark the front edge of the wall at the ends and at any corners and curves. Connect the stakes with mason's string. Use a line level to check the string, and, if necessary, adjust the string so it is level.

3 Dig a trench for the first row of building materials, measuring down from the mason's string to maintain a level trench. Make the trench 6" deeper than the thickness of one layer of building material. For example, if you are using 6"-thick interlocking blocks, make the trench 12" deep.

4 Line the excavation with strips of landscape fabric cut 3 ft. longer than the planned height of the wall. Make sure seams overlap by at least 6".

Building a Retaining Wall Using Interlocking Block

Several styles of interlocking block are available at building and outdoor centers. Most types have a natural rock finish that combines the rough texture of cut stone with the uniform shape and size of concrete blocks.

Interlocking blocks weigh up to 80 lbs. each, so it is a good idea to have helpers when building a retaining wall. Suppliers offer substantial discounts when interlocking block is purchased in large quantities, so you may be able to save money if you coordinate your own project with those of your neighbors.

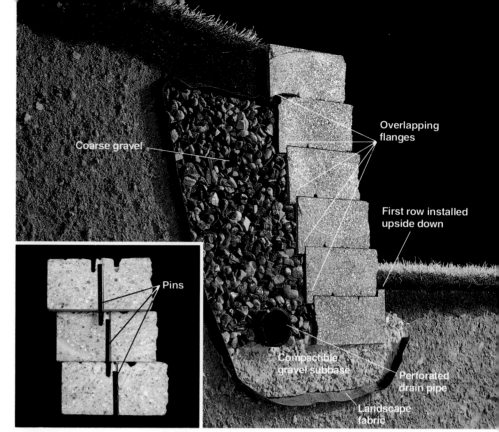

Interlocking wall blocks do not need mortar. Some types are held together with a system of overlapping flanges that automatically set the backward angle (batter) as the blocks are stacked. Other types of blocks use a pinning system (inset).

Tips for Building a Retaining Wall Using Interlocking Block

Make a stepped trench when the ends of a retaining wall must blend into an existing hillside. Retaining walls often are designed so the ends curve or turn back into the slope.

Make half-blocks by scoring full blocks with a circular saw and masonry blade, then breaking the blocks along the scored line with a maul and chisel. Half-blocks are used when making corners, and to ensure that vertical joints between blocks are staggered between rows.

How to Build a Retaining Wall Using Interlocking Block

1 Spread a 6" layer of compactible gravel subbase into the trench and pack thoroughly. A rented tamping machine, sometimes called a "jumping jack," works better than a hand tamper (step 7) for packing the subbase.

2 Lay the first row of blocks into the trench, aligning the front edges with the mason's string. When using flanged blocks, place the first row of blocks upside down and backward. Check the blocks frequently with a level, and adjust, if necessary, by adding or removing subbase material below the blocks.

3 Lay the second row of blocks according to manufacturer's instructions. On flanged blocks, the blocks should be laid so the flanges are tight against the underlying blocks. Check regularly to make sure the blocks are level.

4 Add 6" of gravel behind the blocks, making sure the landscape fabric remains between the gravel and the hillside. Pack the gravel thoroughly with a hand tamper.

5 Place perforated drain pipe on top of the gravel, at least 6" behind wall, with perforations facing down. Make sure that at least one end of the pipe is unobstructed so runoff water can escape (page 17). Lay additional rows of blocks until the wall is about 18" above ground level. Make sure the vertical joints in adjoining rows are offset.

6 Fill behind the wall with coarse gravel, and pack well. Lay the remaining rows of block, except for the cap row, backfilling with gravel and packing with a hand tamper as you go.

7 Before laying the cap blocks, fold the end of the landscape fabric over the gravel backfill. Add a thin layer of topsoil over the fabric, then pack it thoroughly with a hand tamper.

8 Fold any excess landscape fabric back over the soil, then apply construction adhesive to the blocks. Lay the cap blocks in place. Use topsoil to fill in behind the wall and to fill in the trench at the base of the wall. Install sod or other plants, as desired.

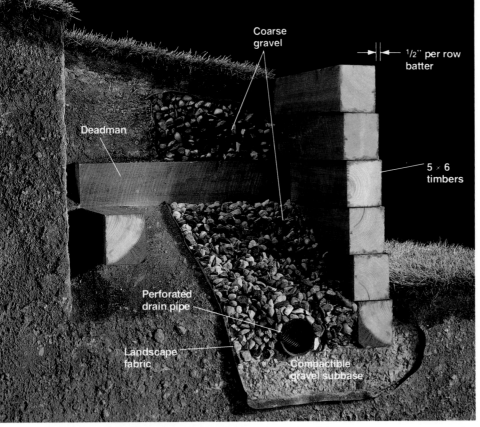

Coarse gravel

Deadman

Perforated drain pipe

Landscape fabric

½" per row batter

5 × 6 timbers

Compactible gravel subbase

Timber retaining walls must be anchored with "deadmen" that extend from the wall back into the soil. Deadmen prevent the wall from sagging under the weight of the soil. For best results with timber retaining walls, create a backward angle (batter) by setting each row of timbers ½" behind the preceding row. The first row of timbers should be buried.

Building a Retaining Wall Using Timbers

Timber walls have a life span of 15 to 20 years if built correctly. Use pressure-treated timbers at least 5 × 6 in size. Smaller timbers are not sturdy enough for retaining walls.

Use a chain saw or reciprocating saw to cut landscape timbers. The pesticides used in treated lumber are toxic, so wear a particle mask, gloves, and long sleeves when cutting or handling pressure-treated lumber. Avoid using old timbers, like discarded railroad ties, that have been soaked in creosote. Creosote can leach into the soil and kill plants.

Before building the retaining wall, prepare the site as directed on page 18.

Tips for Strengthening a Timber Retaining Wall

Timber depth equal to ½ exposed height

Use metal reinforcement bars instead of spikes for extra strength when connecting timbers. Cut 12" to 24" lengths of bar with sharp points, then drive them into pilot holes drilled through the top timber, spaced at 2-ft. intervals. This technique is especially useful if you have heavy, dense soil that drains poorly.

Install vertical anchor posts to reinforce the wall. Space the posts 3 ft. apart, and install them so the buried depth of each post is at least half the exposed height of the wall. Anchor posts are essential if it is not practical to install deadmen (photo, top).

How to Build a Retaining Wall Using Timbers

1 Spread a 6" layer of compactible gravel subbase into the prepared trench, then tamp the subbase and begin laying timbers, following the same techniques as with interlocking blocks (steps 1 to 7, pages 20 to 21). Each row of timbers should be set with a ½" batter, and end joints should be staggered so they do not align.

2 Use 12" galvanized spikes or reinforcement bars to anchor the ends of each timber to the underlying timbers. Stagger the ends of the timbers to form strong corner joints. Drive additional spikes along the length of the timbers at 2-ft. intervals. If you have trouble driving the spikes, drill pilot holes.

3 Install deadmen, spaced 4 ft. apart, midway up the wall. Build the deadmen by joining 3-ft.-long lengths of timber with 12" spikes, then insert the ends through holes cut in the landscape fabric. Anchor deadmen to wall with spikes. Install the remaining rows of timbers, and finish backfilling behind the wall (steps 6 to 8, page 21).

4 Improve drainage by drilling weep holes through the second row of landscape timbers and into the gravel backfill, using a spade bit. Space the holes 4 ft. apart, and angle them upward.

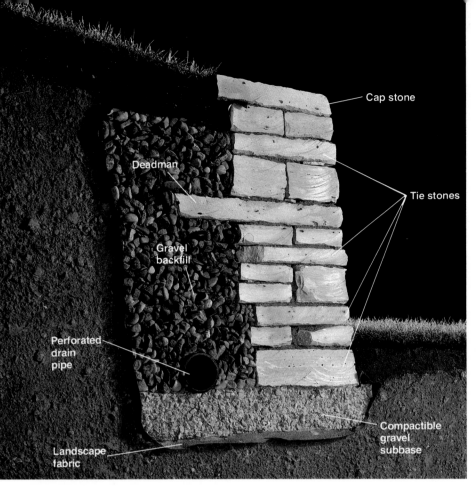

Building a Retaining Wall Using Natural Stone

Retaining walls made from natural cut stone or rubble stone give a traditional, timeless look to a landscape. Natural stone walls usually are laid without mortar, although the last one or two rows can be mortared in place for greater strength. Unlike mortared stone or block walls (pages 26 to 31), unmortared stone walls require no concrete footings.

Before building the retaining wall, prepare the site as directed on page 18. Build the wall by placing the largest stones at the bottom and reserving the smoothest, flattest stones for the corners and the top (cap) row.

Cut stone has flat, smooth surfaces for easy stacking. For a stable retaining wall, alternate rows of "tie stones" that span the entire width of the wall with rows of smaller stones. Install extra-long stones (called deadmen) that extend back into gravel backfill, spaced every 4 to 6 ft.

Retaining Wall Variations Using Rubble Stone

Boulders are large, uncut rocks, usually round in shape. The retaining wall site requires no subbase or backfill: simply dig out the hillside to fit the shape of the boulders and roll them into place. Boulders range in size from about 40 lbs. to several hundred lbs. For heavy boulders, you may want to hire a contractor to deliver and position the rocks.

Field stone refers to any irregular assortment of rough rock. You can gather field stone by hand or buy it from sand-and-gravel companies. Field-stone retaining walls do not need a subbase or backfill; but for better stability, build the wall so it tilts back into the hillside. Pack the open spaces between rocks with rock fragments or soil. If you wish, plant vines or groundcover in the exposed gaps.

How to Build a Retaining Wall Using Cut Stone

1 Spread a 6" layer of compactible gravel subbase into the prepared trench (step 1, page 20), then sort the stones by size and shape so they can be located easily as you build. Make sure you have enough long stones to serve as tie stones, deadmen, and cap stones.

2 Trim irregular stones, if needed, to make them fit solidly into the wall. Always wear eye protection and hearing protectors when cutting stone. Score the stone first using a masonry blade and circular saw set to 1/8" blade depth, then drive a masonry chisel along the scored line until the stone breaks.

Tie stone

Dead man

3 Lay rows of stones, following the same techniques for backfilling as for interlocking blocks (steps 2 to 7, pages 20 to 21). Build a backward slant (batter) into the wall by setting each row of stones about ½" back from the preceding row. For stability, work tie stones and deadmen into the wall at frequent intervals.

Cap stone

4 Before laying the cap row of stones, mix mortar according to manufacturer's directions and apply a thick bed along the tops of the installed stones, keeping the mortar at least 6" from the front face of the wall. Lay the cap stones, and press them into the mortar. Because the mortar is not visible, this technique is called "blind mortaring." Finish backfilling behind the wall (step 8, page 21).

Building a Free-standing Wall

A free-standing wall serves the same function as a hedge or fence, but is much sturdier. Walls are popular in areas where growing shrubs and hedges is difficult. Free-standing walls can train climbing plants or support trellises or container plants. Low walls may be used as garden benches.

Most free-standing walls are built by mortaring concrete block, brick, or natural stone. The following pages show how to build a concrete block wall, but similar techniques can be used for any mortared wall.

Free-standing walls also can be built from unmortared stones, using techniques similar to those used in building a stone retaining wall (pages 24 to 25).

Limit your walls to 3 ft. in height. Taller walls need deep footings and extra reinforcement. Increase privacy by adding a trellis to the wall (photo, top left). Many local Building Codes limit the total height of the wall and trellis to 6 ft.

A stucco finish and lattice panels turn a plain concrete block wall into a durable, attractive privacy wall. See pages 32 to 33 for these finishing techniques.

Other Options for Finishing a Concrete Block Wall

Stone Veneer (sometimes called cultured stone) copies the look of natural stone at a fraction of the cost. Available in dozens of different styles, stone veneer kits come with an assortment of flat pieces and corner pieces. The veneer is held in place with a layer of standard mortar (page 33).

Decorative block adds visual interest to a plain concrete block wall. Check with your local building inspector before adding block to a wall, since the added height may require extra reinforcement. Decorative block also may be used to build an entire wall.

Everything You Need:

Tools: tape measure, rake, hammer, level, shovel, wheelbarrow, old paint brush, chalk line, trowel, rubber gloves, pencil, line level, masonry chisel, masonry hammer, V-shaped mortar tool, garden hoe, level.

Materials: rope, stakes, 2 × 6 lumber, compactible gravel subbase, reinforcement rods, oil, premixed concrete, concrete blocks, sheet plastic, 3/8"-thick wood strips, mortar mix, mason's string.

How to Install a Footing for a Free-standing Wall

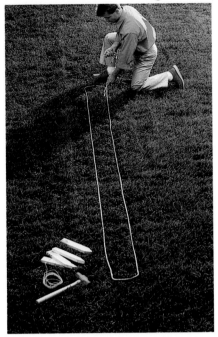

1 Lay out the rough position of the wall, using a rope.

2 Outline the wall footing, using stakes and mason's string. Check the string with a line level and adjust as needed. The footing should be twice as wide as the planned wall, and should extend 1 ft. beyond each end.

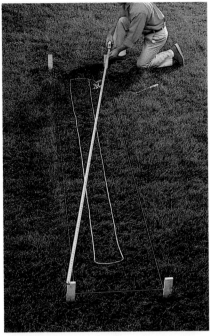

3 Measure the diagonals to make sure the outline is square, and adjust as necessary. Dig a 1-ft.-deep trench for the footing, using the strings as a guide. Make sure the bottom of the trench is roughly level.

4 Lay a 6" layer of compactible gravel subbase into the trench. Tamp the subbase thoroughly (page 21). NOTE: Follow local Building Code guidelines for footing depth.

5 Build a wood form using 2 × 6 lumber, and set it in the trench. Add or remove subbase material to level the form. Drive stakes along the outside of the form to anchor it.

6 Lay reinforcement bars inside the form to make the footing more crack-resistant. Set the bars on 2 × 4 scraps, a few inches inside the form. Coat the inside of the form with oil for easy removal.

(continued next page)

How to Install a Footing for a Free-standing Wall (continued)

7 Fill the form up to the top of the boards with concrete. Work the concrete with a shovel just enough to remove air pockets.

8 Smooth off (screed) the surface of the concrete by dragging a short 2 × 4 along the top of the form. Add concrete to any low areas, and screed again.

9 When concrete is hard to the touch, cover it with plastic and let it cure for 2 or 3 days. When surface has cured, pry the forms loose with a shovel.

How to Build a Free-standing Wall Using Concrete Block

Reference lines

1 Test-fit a row of blocks on the footing, using smooth-sided end blocks at the ends. You may need to use half-blocks on one end to achieve the desired wall length. Use 3/8"-thick wood strips or dowels as spacers to maintain an even gap for mortar between the blocks.

2 Draw pencil lines on the concrete to mark the ends of the test-fitted row. Extend the line well past the edges of the block. Use a chalk line to snap reference lines on each side of the footing, 3" from the blocks. These reference lines will serve as a guide when setting the blocks into mortar.

3 Remove the blocks and set them nearby. Mix mortar in a wheelbarrow or large pail, following manufacturer's directions. Mortar should be moist enough to hold its shape when squeezed.

4 Trowel thick lines of mortar, slightly wider and longer than the base of the end block, onto the center of the footing. If the footing has cured for over a week, dampen it before mortaring.

TIP: When positioning concrete blocks, make sure the side with the wider flanges is facing upward. The wider flanges provide more surface for applying mortar.

Wider flanges

5 Set an end block into the mortar, so the end is aligned with the pencil mark on the footing. Set a level on top of the block, then tap the block with a trowel handle until it is level. Use the chalkline as a reference point for keeping the block in line.

6 Apply mortar, then set and level the block at the opposite end of the footing. Stake a mason's string even with the top outside corners of the blocks. Check the string with a line level, then adjust the blocks to align with the string. Remove excess mortar, and fill the gaps beneath the end blocks (inset).

(continued next page)

7 Apply mortar to the vertical flanges on one side of a standard block (inset) and to the footing, using a trowel. Set the block next to the end block, leaving a 3/8" layer of mortar between blocks. Tap the block into position with a trowel handle, using the string as a guide to align the block.

8 Install the remaining blocks, working back and forth from opposite ends. Be careful to maintain 3/8" joints to ensure that the last block in the row will fit. Make sure the row is level and straight by aligning the blocks with the mason's string and checking them with a carpenter's level.

9 At the middle of the row, apply mortar to the vertical flanges on both sides of the last block, then slide the block down into place. Align the last block with the mason's string.

10 Apply a 1" layer of mortar to the top flanges of the end blocks. Scrape off any mortar that falls onto the footing.

11 Begin laying the second row. Use half-size end blocks to create staggered vertical joints. Check with a straightedge to make sure the new blocks are aligned with the bottom blocks.

VARIATION: If your wall has a corner, begin the second row with a full-sized end block that spans the vertical joint formed where two sides of the wall meet. This creates staggered vertical joints.

12 Insert a nail into the wet mortar at each end of the wall. Attach a mason's string to one nail, then stretch the string up over the corners of the end blocks and tie it to the nail at the opposite end.

13 Install the second row of blocks, using the same method as with the first row. When the second row is completed, remove the nails and mason's string. Scrape off excess mortar, and finish the joints with a V-shaped mortar tool. Install each additional row of blocks by repeating steps 11 to 13. Finish the joints as each row of blocks is completed.

14 Complete the wall with a row of cap blocks. Cap blocks are very heavy, and must be laid gently to keep mortar from being squeezed out. If you are adding lattice panels to the top of the wall, insert J-bolts into the joints between the cap blocks while mortar is still wet (page 32).

How to Add Lattice Panels to a Block Wall

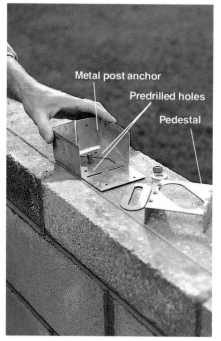

Metal post anchor
Predrilled holes
Pedestal

1 While mortar is still wet, install 3/8"-diameter J-bolts into the center of the cap row joints at post locations. About 1" of the bolt should protrude. Pack mortar around the bolt and let it harden. (If mortar already has hardened, see OPTION, step 2.)

2 Align and attach a metal post anchor at each post location. Slip an oval washer over each J-bolt, then attach a nut. OPTION: Attach metal post anchors by driving self-tapping masonry anchors through the predrilled holes in the bottom of the post anchor.

3 Set a metal pedestal into each anchor. The top of the J-bolt should be below the pedestal.

4 Cut a 4 × 4 post for each anchor. Set the post on the pedestal, then bend the open flange up against the post. Make sure the post is plumb, then attach it with 6d galvanized nails.

5 Assemble and install lattice panels between posts. Most lattice panels are 8 ft. long, and can be cut to fit if your posts are spaced less than 8 ft. apart.

How to Finish a Block Wall with Stucco

1 Attach wire lath to the entire surface of all wall faces, using self-tapping masonry anchors. Lath provides a surface for application of stucco or mortar (step 1, below).

2 Mix stucco, using a ratio of 3 parts sand and 2 parts portland cement, adding enough water so the mixture holds its shape when squeezed. Trowel a 3/8"-thick layer directly onto the metal lath. Scratch grooves into the surface of the stucco, then let the coat cure for two days. Dampen a few times daily.

3 Apply a second 3/8" layer of the same stucco mixture over the first coat. Do not scratch this layer. Let stucco cure for two days. Dampen a few times daily.

4 Mix a finish stucco coat, using 1 part lime, 3 parts sand, and 6 parts white cement. Dampen walls, and dab a finish coat onto the wall, using a whisk broom.

5 Flatten the surface of the finish coat with a trowel. Dampen the wall daily for three or four days to complete the curing.

How to Apply Stone Veneer to a Block Wall

1 Prepare wall with wire lath (step 1, above), then apply a 1/2"-thick layer of standard mortar to the wall. Scratch grooves into the damp mortar, using the trowel tip, then allow to dry overnight. Beginning at the bottom of the wall, apply mortar to the back of each veneer piece, then press it onto the wall with a twisting motion. Keep a 1/2" gap between pieces.

2 After mortar has dried for a day, fill the joints with fresh mortar, using a mortar bag. Use a V-shaped mortar tool to finish the joints (step 13, page 31).

Flagstone walkways combine charm with durability, and work well in both casual and formal settings. Also a popular material for patios, flagstone can be set in sand, or it can be mortared in place. See pages 38 to 39.
TIP: Prevent damage to the edging material by trimming near the walkway with a line-feed trimmer instead of a mower.

Building Walkways & Paths

Walkways and paths serve as "hallways" between heavily used areas of your yard, and can be used to direct traffic toward a favorite landscape feature, like a pond. Walkways also create a visual corridor that directs the eye from one area to another.

Curved paths give a softer, more relaxed look to a landscape, but straight or angular paths and walkways fit well in contemporary landscape designs.

Garden paths often are made from loose materials, like crushed rock or bark, held in place by edging. Walkways are more durable when made from stone or brick paving materials set in sand or mortar. Poured concrete sidewalks are practical and the most durable, but unless you have a lot of experience pouring and curing concrete, do not attempt to build them yourself. Most paving techniques used in patio construction (pages 50 to 59) can be used for walkways as well.

Everything You Need:

Tools: tape measure, spade, garden rake, rubber mallet, circular saw with masonry blade, masonry chisel, masonry hammer.

Materials: landscape fabric, garden hose, edging material (page 36), walkway surface materials, galvanized screws, 2 × 6 lumber. Added supplies for mortared brick walkways: mortar, mortar bag, V-shaped mortar tool, trowel.

Loose materials, such as gravel, crushed rock, wood chips and bark, make informal, inexpensive pathways that are well suited for light-traffic areas. Build loose-material paths with the surface material slightly above ground level, to keep it from being washed away.

Brick pavers provide stately charm to a main walkway, making a house more appealing from the street. Because pavers are very durable, they are ideal for heavy-traffic areas. Brick pavers can be set in sand, or mortared in place over an old concrete surface. Pavers used for mortared walkways often are thinner than those designed for sand installation.

Tips for Building a Walkway

Use a sod cutter to strip grass from your pathway site. Available at most rental centers, sod cutters excavate to a very even depth. The cut sod can be replanted in other parts of your lawn.

Install stakes and strings when laying out straight walkways made from stone paving materials, and measure from the strings to ensure straight sides and uniform excavation depth.

Brick edging makes a good boundary for both straight and curved paths made from loose materials. See page 37.

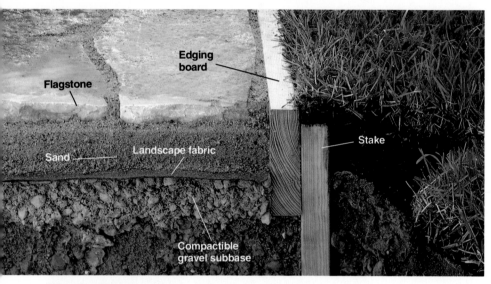

Wood edging makes a sturdy border for straight walkways made from flagstone or brick pavers set in sand. See pages 38 to 39.

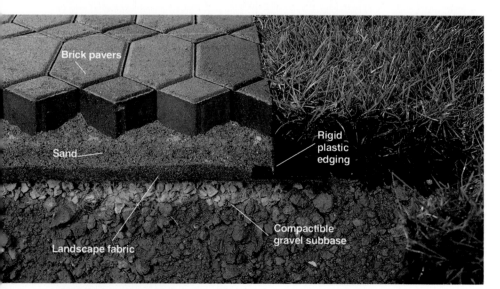

Rigid plastic edging installs easily, and works well for both curved and straight walkways made from paving stones or brick pavers set in sand. See pages 50 to 59.

Types of Edging

Use edging to keep walkway materials in place. Consider cost, appearance, flexibility, and ease of installation when selecting an edging type.

Brick edging set in soil is good for casual, lightly traveled pathways, but should be used only in soil that is dense and well drained. (Bricks in loose or swampy soil will not hold their position). Bricks can be set vertically, or tilted at an angle to make a saw-tooth pattern. Brick pavers also can be mortared to the sides of an old sidewalk to create a border for a new surface (pages 40 to 41).

Wood edging made from pressure-treated lumber, red-wood, or cedar is inexpensive and easy to install. The tops of the boards are left exposed to create an attractive border. The wood edging boards are held in place by attaching them to recessed wood stakes spaced every 12" along the outside of the edging.

Rigid plastic edging is inconspicuous, durable, and easy to install. It was developed as an edging for brick pavers set in sand. Rigid plastic edging is held in place by the weight of the soil and with galvanized spikes driven through the back flange. Rolled vinyl edging is used most often to make boundaries for planting areas, but also works as an edging for casual walkways. It is inexpensive and very flexible.

How to Build a Path Using Loose Materials & Brick Edging

1 Outline the path using a garden hose or rope, then excavate the site to a depth of 2" to 3", using a spade, hoe, or a rented sod cutter (page 35). Rake the site smooth.

2 Dig narrow edging trenches about 2" deeper than the path site along both edges of the excavation, using a spade or hoe.

3 Lay landscaping fabric between the edging trenches to prevent weeds from growing. Overlap sheets by at least 6".

4 Set bricks on end into the edging trenches, with the tops slightly above ground level. Pack soil behind and beneath each brick, adjusting the bricks, if necessary, to keep the rows even.

5 Finish the path by spreading loose material (gravel, crushed rock, bark, or wood chips) between the rows of edging bricks. Level the surface with a garden rake. The loose material should be slightly above ground level. Tap each brick lightly on the inside face to help set it into the soil. Inspect and adjust the bricks yearly, adding new loose material as needed.

How to Build a Flagstone Walkway Using Wood Edging

1 Outline the walkway site and excavate to a depth of 6". Allow enough room for the edging and stakes (step 2). For straight walkways, use stakes and strings to maintain a uniform outline (page 35). Add a 2" layer of compactible gravel subbase, using a rake to smooth the surface.

2 Install 2 × 6 edging made from pressure-treated lumber around the sides of the site. Drive 12" stakes on the outside of the edging, spaced 12" apart. Tops of the stakes should be below ground level. Attach the edging to the stakes using galvanized screws.

3 Test-fit the flagstones to find an efficient, attractive arrangement of stones. Arrange the stones to minimize the number of cuts needed. Leave a gap between stones that is at least 3/8", but no more than 2" wide. Use a pencil to mark stones for cutting, then remove the stones and set them nearby.

4 Cut flagstones by scoring along the marked lines with a circular saw and masonry blade set to 1/8" blade depth. Set a piece of wood under the stone, just inside the scored line, then use a masonry chisel and hammer to strike along the scored line until the stone breaks.

Flagstone thickness

Width of walkway

5 Lay sheets of landscape fabric over the walkway site to prevent plants and grass from growing up between the stones. (Omit the landscape fabric if you want to plant grass or ground cover to fill the cracks.) Spread a 2" layer of sand over the landscape fabric to serve as the base for the flagstones.

6 Make a "screed" for smoothing the sand by notching the ends of a short 2 × 6 to fit inside the edging (see inset). The depth of the notches should equal the thickness of the stones, usually about 2". Screed the base by pulling the 2 × 6 from one end of the walkway to the other. Add more sand as needed until the base is smooth.

7 Beginning at one corner of the walkway, lay the flagstones onto the sand base so the gap between stones is at least 3/8", but no more than 2". If needed, add or remove sand beneath stones to level them. Set the stones by tapping them with a rubber mallet or a length of 2 × 4.

8 Fill the gaps between stones with sand. (Use soil if you are planting grass or ground cover in the cracks.) Pack the sand with your fingers or a piece of scrap wood, then spray the walkway lightly with water to help the sand settle. Add new sand as necessary until gaps are filled.

How to Resurface a Sidewalk Using Mortared Brick Pavers

1 Select a paver pattern (page 51), then dig a trench around the concrete, slightly wider than the thickness of one paver. Dig the trench so it is about 3½" below the concrete surface. Soak the pavers with water before mortaring. Dry pavers absorb moisture, weakening the mortar strength.

2 Sweep the old concrete, then hose off the surface and sides with water to clear away dirt and debris. Mix a small batch of mortar according to manufacturer's directions. For convenience, place the mortar on a scrap of plywood.

3 Install edging bricks by applying a ½" layer of mortar to the side of the concrete slab and to one side of each brick. Set bricks into the trench, against the concrete. Brick edging should be ½" higher than the thickness of the brick pavers.

4 Finish the joints on the edging bricks with a V-shaped mortar tool (step 9), then mix and apply a ½"-thick bed of mortar to one end of the sidewalk, using a trowel. Mortar hardens very quickly, so work in sections no larger than 4 sq. ft.

5 Make a "screed" for smoothing mortar by notching the ends of a short 2 × 4 to fit between the edging bricks (page 39). Depth of the notches should equal the thickness of the pavers. Drag the screed across the mortar bed until the mortar is smooth.

6 Lay the paving bricks one at a time into the mortar, maintaining a 1/2" gap between pavers. (A piece of scrap plywood works well as a spacing guide.) Set the pavers by tapping them lightly with a rubber mallet.

7 As each section of pavers is completed, check with a straightedge to make sure the tops of the pavers are even.

8 When all the pavers are installed, use a mortar bag to fill the joints between the pavers with fresh mortar. Work in 4-sq.-ft. sections, and avoid getting mortar on the tops of the pavers.

9 Use a V-shaped mortar tool to finish the joints as you complete each 4-sq.-ft. section. For best results, finish the longer joints first, then the shorter joints. Use a trowel to remove excess mortar.

10 Let the mortar dry for a few hours, then scrub the pavers with a coarse rag and water. Cover the walkway with plastic and let the mortar cure for at least 24 hours. Remove plastic, but do not walk on the pavers for at least three days.

Riser

Tread

Simple garden steps can be built by making a series of concrete platforms framed with 5 × 6 timbers. Garden steps have shorter vertical risers and deeper horizontal treads than house stairs. Risers for garden stairs should be no more than 6", and treads should be at least 11" deep.

Building Garden Steps

Garden steps make sloping yards safer and more accessible. They also add visual interest by introducing new combinations of materials into your landscape design.

You can build garden steps with a wide variety of materials, including flagstone, brick, timbers, concrete block, or poured concrete. Whatever materials you use, make sure the steps are level and firmly anchored. They should be easy to climb and have a rough texture for good traction.

Everything You Need:

Tools: chain saw or reciprocating saw with 12" wood-cutting blade, tape measure, level, masonry hammer, shovel, drill with 1" spade bit and bit extension, rake, wheelbarrow, hoe, concrete float, edging tool, stiff brush.

Materials: 2 × 4 lumber, 5 × 6 landscape timbers, mason's string, 3/4" I.D. (interior diameter) black pipe, 12" galvanized spikes, premixed concrete, compactible gravel subbase, seed gravel (1/2" maximum diameter), sheet plastic, burlap.

Tips for Mixing Concrete

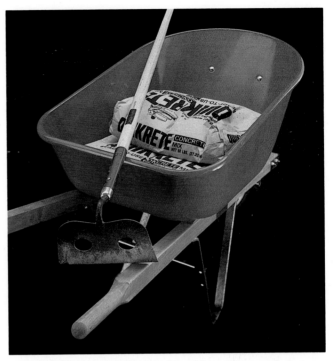

For large amounts (more than 1/2 cubic yard), mix your own dry ingredients in a wheelbarrow or rented mixer. Use a ratio of 1 part portland cement (A), 2 parts sand (B), and 3 parts gravel (C). See page 12 to estimate the amount of concrete needed.

For small amounts (less than 1/2 cubic yard), buy premixed bags of dry concrete. A 60-lb. bag of concrete creates about 1/2 cubic foot of concrete. A special hoe with holes in the blade is useful for mixing concrete.

Tips for Building Garden Steps

1/8" downward pitch per foot

Build a slight downward pitch into outdoor steps so water will drain off without puddling Do not exceed a pitch of 1/8" per foot.

Order custom-cut timbers to reduce installation time if the dimensions of each step are identical. Some building supply centers charge a small fee for custom-cutting timbers.

How to Plan Garden Steps

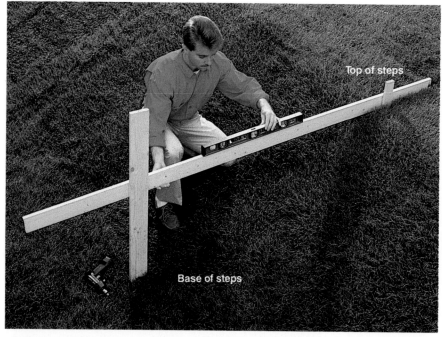

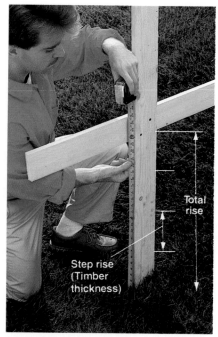

1 Drive a tall stake into the ground at the base of the stairway site. Adjust the stake so it is exactly plumb. Drive a shorter stake at the top of the site. Position a long, straight 2 × 4 against the stakes, with one end touching the ground next to the top stake. Adjust the 2 × 4 so it is level, then attach it to the stakes with screws. (For long spans, use a mason's string instead of a 2 × 4.)

2 Measure from the ground to the bottom of the 2 × 4 to find the total vertical **rise** of the stairway. Divide the rise by the actual thickness of the timbers (6" if using 5 × 6 timbers) to find the number of steps required. Round off fractions to the nearest full number.

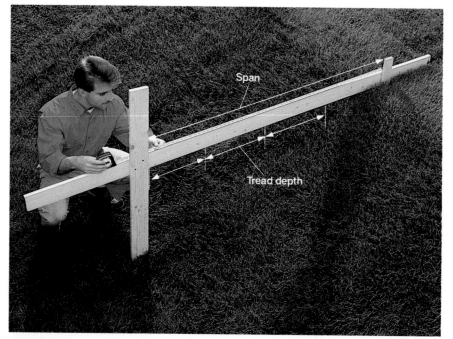

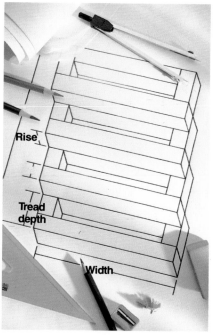

3 Measure along the 2 × 4 between the stakes to find the total horizontal **span**. Divide the span by the number of steps to find the depth of each step tread. If depth is less than 11", revise the step layout to extend the depth of the step treads.

4 Make a sketch of the step site, showing rise, tread depth, and width of each step. Remember that actual timber dimensions may vary from the nominal measurements.

How to Build Garden Steps Using Timbers & Concrete

1 Mark the sides of the step site with stakes and string. The stakes should be positioned at the front edge of the bottom step and the back edge of the top step.

Tread depth

2 Add the width of a timber (5") to the tread depth, then measure back this distance from the stakes and drive additional stakes to mark the back edge of the first step. Connect these stakes with string to mark the digging area for the first step.

3 Excavate for the first step, creating a flat bed with a very slight forward slope, no more than 1/8" from back to front. Front of excavation should be no more than 2" deep. Tamp the soil firmly.

4 For each step, use a chain saw or reciprocating saw to cut a front timber equal to the step width, a back timber 10" shorter, and two side timbers equal to the tread depth.

(continued next page)

5 Arrange the timbers to form the step frame, and end-nail them together with 12" spikes.

6 Set the timber frame in position. Use a carpenter's square to make sure the frame is square, and adjust as necessary. Drill two 1" guide holes in the front timber and the back timber, 1 ft. from the ends, using a spade bit and bit extension.

7 Anchor the steps to the ground by driving a 2½-ft. length of ¾" pipe through each guide hole until the pipe is flush with the timber. When pipes are driven, make sure the frame is level from side to side and has the proper forward pitch. Excavate for the next step, making sure the bottom of the excavation is even with top edge of the installed timbers.

Drive pipes here

8 Build another step frame and position it in the excavation so the front timber is directly over the rear timber on the first frame. Nail the steps together with three 12" spikes, then drill guide holes and drive two pipes through only the back timber to anchor the second frame.

9 Continue digging and installing the remaining frames until the steps reach full height. The back of the last step should be at ground level.

10 Staple plastic over the timbers to protect them from wet concrete. Cut away the plastic so it does not overhang into the frame opening.

11 Pour a 2" layer of compactible gravel subbase into each frame, and use a 2 × 4 to smooth it out.

12 Mix concrete in a wheelbarrow, adding just enough water so the concrete holds its shape when sliced with a trowel. NOTE: To save time and labor, you can have ready-mix concrete delivered to the site. Ready-mix companies will deliver concrete in amounts as small as $1/3$ cubic yard (enough for three steps of the type shown here).

13 Shovel concrete into the bottom frame, flush with the top of the timbers. Work the concrete lightly with a garden rake to help remove air bubbles, but do not overwork the concrete.

(continued next page)

14 Smooth (screed) the concrete by dragging a 2 x 4 across the top of the frame. If necessary, add concrete to low areas and screed again until the surface is smooth and free of low spots.

15 While the concrete is still wet, "seed" it by scattering mixed gravel onto the surface. Sand-and-gravel suppliers and garden centers sell colorful gravel designed for seeding. For best results, select a mixture with stones no larger than 1/2" in diameter.

16 Press the seeded gravel into the surface of the concrete, using a concrete float, until the tops of the stones are flush with the surface of the concrete. Remove any concrete that spills over the edges of the frame, using a trowel.

17 Pour concrete into remaining steps, screeding and seeding each step before moving on to the next. For a neater appearance, use an edging tool (inset) to smooth the cracks between the timbers and the concrete as each step is finished.

18 When the sheen disappears from the poured concrete (4 to 6 hours after pouring), use a float to smooth out any high or low spots in each step. Be careful not to force seeded gravel too far into the concrete. Let the concrete dry overnight.

19 After concrete has dried overnight, apply a fine mist of water to the surface, then scrub it with a stiff brush to expose the seeded gravel.

VARIATION: To save time and money, skip the seeding procedure. To create a nonslip surface on smooth concrete, draw a stiff-bristled brush or broom once across the concrete while it is still wet.

20 Remove the plastic from the timbers, and cover the concrete with burlap. Allow concrete to cure for several days, spraying it occasionally with water to ensure even curing. NOTE: Concrete residue can be cleaned from timbers, using a solution of 5% muriatic acid and water.

Building a Patio

A patio can serve as the visual centerpiece of your yard and as the focus of your outdoor life-style. To be functional, a patio should be as large as a standard room—100 square feet or more.

Brick pavers are the most common material used for patios, but you can also build a patio with flagstone, following the same methods used for flagstone walkways (pages 34 to 41).

The most important part of a patio project is excavating and creating a flat base with the proper slope for drainage. This work is easier if you build your patio on a site that is relatively flat and level. On a hilly, uneven yard, you may be able to create flat space for a patio by building a retaining wall terrace (pages 16 to 25).

Everything You Need

Tools: tape measure, carpenter's level, shovel, line level, rake, hand tamper, tamping machine.

Materials: stakes, mason's string, compactible gravel subbase, rigid plastic edging, landscape fabric, sand, pavers, 1"-thick pipes.

Interlocking brick pavers come in many shapes and colors. Two popular paver styles include Uni-Decor™ (left) and Symmetry™ (right). Patios made with interlocking pavers may have a border row made from standard brick pavers (page opposite).

Common Paving Patterns for Standard Brick Pavers

Standard brick pavers can be arranged in several different patterns, including: (A) running bond, (B) jack-on-jack, (C) herringbone, and (D) basketweave. Jack-on-jack and basketweave patterns require fewer cut pavers along the edges. Standard pavers have spacing lugs on the sides that automatically set the joints at ⅛" width. See page 14 to estimate the number of pavers you will need for your patio.

Installation Variations for Brick Pavers

Sand-set: Pavers rest on a 1" bed of sand laid over a 4" compactible gravel subbase. Rigid plastic edging holds the sand base in place. Joints are ⅛" wide, and are packed with sand, which holds the pavers securely yet allows them to shift slightly as temperatures change.

Dry mortar: Installation is similar to sand-set patio, but joints are ⅜" wide, and are packed with a mixture of sand and mortar, soaked with water, and finished with a V-shaped mortar tool. A dry-mortar patio has a more finished masonry look than a sand-set patio, but the joints must be repaired periodically.

Wet mortar: This method often is used when pavers are installed over an old concrete patio or sidewalk (see pages 40 to 41). Joints are ½" wide. Wet mortar installation can also be used with flagstone. For edging on a wet-mortar patio, use rigid plastic edging or paver bricks set on end.

How to Build a Sand-set Patio with Brick Pavers

1 To find exact patio measurements and reduce the number of cut bricks needed, test-fit perpendicular rows of brick pavers on a flat surface, like a driveway. Lay two rows to reach the rough length and width of your patio, then measure the rows to find the exact size. (For a dry-mortar patio, put 3/8" spaces between pavers when test-fitting the rows.)

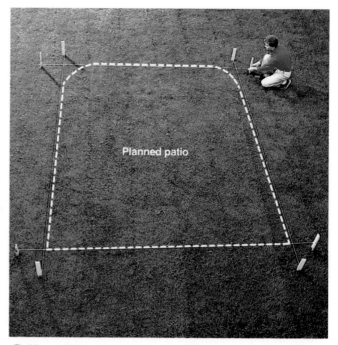

2 Use stakes and mason's string to mark out a rectangle that matches the length and width of your patio. Drive the stakes so they are at least 1 ft. outside the site of the planned patio. The intersecting strings mark the actual corners of the patio site.

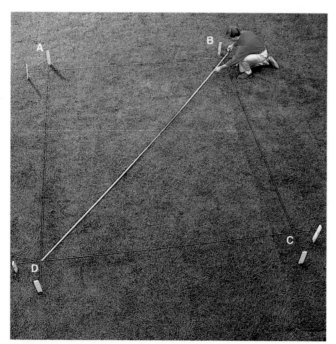

3 Check the rectangle for squareness by measuring the diagonals (A-C, B-D). If the rectangle is square, the diagonals will have the same measurement. If not, adjust the stakes and strings until the diagonals are equal. The strings will serve as a reference for excavating the patio site.

4 Using a line level as a guide, adjust one of the strings until it is level. When the string is level, mark its height on the stakes at each end of the string.

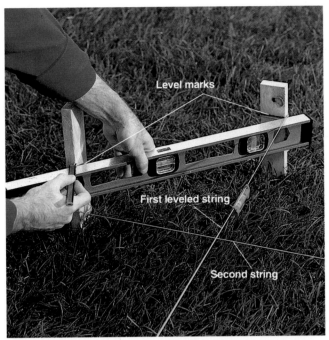

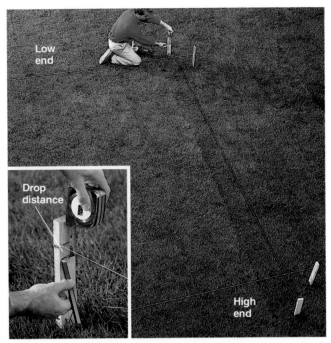

5 To adjust each remaining string so it is level and even with the first string, use a carpenter's level as a guide for marking adjacent stakes, then adjust the strings to the reference marks. Use a line level to make sure all strings are level.

6 To ensure good drainage, choose one end of the patio as the low end. (For most patios, this will be the end farthest from the house.) Measure from the high end to the low end (in feet), then multiply this number by 1/8" to find the proper drop distance. Measure down from the level marks on the low-end stakes, and mark the drop distance (inset).

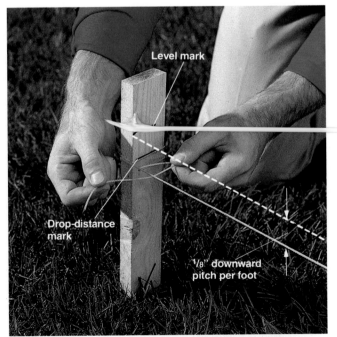

7 Lower the strings at the low-end stakes so the strings are even with the drop-distance marks. Keep all strings in place as a guide while excavating the site and installing the edging.

8 Remove all sod inside the strings and 6" beyond the edges of the planned patio. NOTE: If your patio will have rounded corners, use a garden hose or rope to outline the excavation.

(continued next page)

How to Build a Sand-set Patio with Brick Pavers (continued)

9 Starting at the outside edge, excavate the patio site so it is at least 5" deeper than the thickness of the pavers. For example, if your pavers are 1³/4" thick, excavate to a depth of 6 ³/4". Try to follow the slope of the side strings, and periodically use a long 2 × 4 to check the bottom of the excavation site for high and low spots.

10 Pour compactible gravel subbase over the patio site, then rake it into a smooth layer at least 4" deep. The thickness of the subbase layer may vary to compensate for unevenness in the excavation. Use a long 2 × 4 to check the surface of the subbase for high and low spots, and add or remove compactible gravel as needed.

11 Pack the subbase using a tamping machine until the surface is firm and flat. Check the slope of the subbase by measuring down from the side strings (see step 14). The space between the strings and the subbase should be equal at all points.

12 Cut strips of landscape fabric and lay them over the subbase to prevent weeds from growing up through the patio. Make sure the strips overlap by at least 6".

13 Install rigid plastic edging around the edges of the patio below the reference strings. Anchor the edging by driving galvanized spikes through the predrilled holes and into the subbase. To allow for possible adjustments, drive only enough spikes to keep the edging in place.

14 Check the slope by measuring from the string to the top of the edging at several points. The measurement should be the same at each point. If not, adjust the edging by adding or removing sub-base material under the landscape fabric until the edging follows the slope of the strings.

15 For curves and rounded patio corners, use rigid plastic edging with notches on the outside flange. It may be necessary to anchor each section of edging with spikes to hold curved edging in place.

16 Remove the reference strings, then set 1"-thick pipes or wood strips across the patio area, spaced every 6 ft., to serve as depth spacers for laying the sand base.

(continued next page)

How to Build a Sand-set Patio with Brick Pavers (continued)

17 Lay a 1"-thick layer of sand over the landscape fabric and smooth it out with a garden rake. Sand should just cover the tops of the depth spacers.

18 Water the sand thoroughly, and pack it lightly with a hand tamper.

19 Screed the sand to an even layer by resting a long 2 × 4 on the spacers embedded in the sand and drawing the 2 × 4 across the spacers using a sawing motion. Add extra sand to fill footprints and low areas, then water, tamp, and screed the sand again until it is smooth and firmly packed.

20 Remove the embedded spacers along the sides of the patio base, then fill the grooves with sand and pat them smooth with the hand tamper.

21 Lay the first border paver in one corner of the patio. Make sure the paver rests firmly against the rigid plastic edging.

22 Lay the next border paver so it is tight against the previous paver. Set the pavers by tapping them into the sand with a mallet. Use the depth of the first paver as a guide for setting the remaining pavers.

23 Working outward from the corner, install 2-ft.-wide sections of border pavers and interior pavers, following the desired pattern. Keep the joints between pavers very tight. Set each paver by tapping it with the mallet.

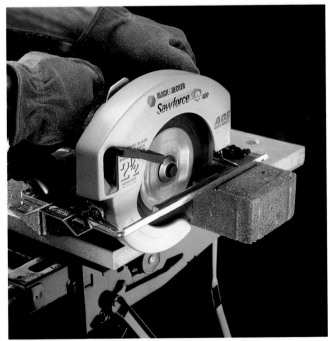

24 If your patio pattern requires that you cut pavers, use a circular saw with a diamond-tipped blade or masonry blade to saw them to size. Always wear eye protection and work gloves when cutting pavers.

25 After each section of pavers is set, use a straightedge to make sure the pavers are flat. Make adjustments by tapping high pavers deeper into the sand, or by removing low pavers and adding a thin layer of extra sand underneath them.

(continued next page)

26 Remove the remaining spacers when the installed surface gets near to them. Fill the gaps left by the spacers with loose sand, and pat the surface smooth with a hand tamper (inset).

27 Continue installing 2-ft.-wide sections of border pavers and interior pavers. As you approach the opposite side of the patio, reposition the rigid plastic edging, if necessary, so full-sized pavers will fit without cutting.

28 At rounded corners and curves, install border pavers in a fan pattern with even gaps between the pavers. Gentle curves may accommodate full-sized border pavers, but for sharper bends you may need to mark and trim wedge-shaped border pavers to make them fit.

29 Lay the remaining interior pavers. Where partial pavers are needed, hold a paver over the gap, and mark the cut with a pencil and straightedge. Cut pavers with a circular saw and masonry blade (step 24). After all pavers are installed, drive in the remaining edging spikes and pack soil behind the edging.

30 Use a long 2 × 4 to check the entire patio for flatness. Adjust uneven pavers by tapping high pavers deeper into the sand, or by removing low pavers and adding a thin layer of extra sand underneath them. After adjusting bricks, use a mason's string to check the rows for straightness.

31 Spread a 1/2" layer of sand over the patio. Use the tamping machine to compress the entire patio and pack sand into the joints.

32 Sweep up the loose sand, then soak the patio area thoroughly to settle the sand in the joints. Let the surface dry completely. If necessary, repeat step 31 until the gaps between pavers are packed tightly with sand.

Dry-mortar option: For a finished masonry look, install pavers with a 3/8" gap between bricks. Instead of sand, fill gaps with a dry mixture made from 4 parts sand and 1 part dry mortar. After spreading the dry mixture and tamping the patio, sprinkle surface with water. While mortar joints are damp, finish them with a V-shaped mortar tool (shown above). After mortar hardens, scrub pavers with water and a coarse rag.

Building a Wood Fence

A fence is as much a part of the neighborhood's landscape as your own. For this reason, local Building Codes and neighborhood covenants may restrict how and where you can build a fence.

In residential areas, for example, privacy fences usually are limited to 6 ft. in height. Remember that the fence you build to give you privacy also will obstruct the view of neighbors. Avoid hard feelings by discussing your plans with neighbors before building a fence. If you are willing to compromise, you may find that neighbors will share the work and expense.

Determine the exact property boundaries before you lay out the fence lines. You may need to call the city or county surveyor to pinpoint these boundaries. To avoid disputes, position your fence at least 6" inside the property line, even if there are no setback regulations (page 7).

To ensure sturdy construction, all screening fences should have posts anchored with concrete footings. When buying posts, remember that footing depths are determined by your local Building Code. In cold climates, local Codes may require that fence footings extend past the winter frost line.

Many homes have chain-link fences that provide security but are not very attractive. To soften the look of chain-link, plant climbing vines, shrubs, or tall perennials against the fence.

Everything You Need:

Tools: tape measure, line level, plumb bob, rented power auger, circular saw, pencil, shovel, hammer, cordless screwdriver, paint brush, pressure sprayer.

Materials: 4 x 4 fence posts, stakes, mason's string, masking tape, coarse gravel, 2 x 4 lumber, premixed concrete, fence panels or boards, galvanized fence brackets, 4d galvanized nails, 3" galvanized utility screws, preassembled gate, gate hinges and latch, post caps, galvanized casing nails, liquid sealer-preservative.

How to Install Fence Posts

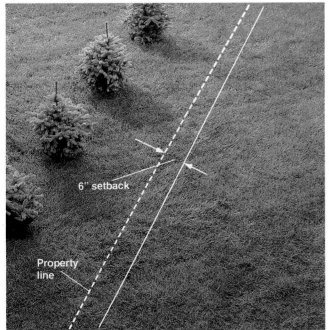

1 Determine the exact property lines if your fence will adjoin your neighbor's property. Plan your fence line with a setback of at least 6" from the legal property line. (Local regulations may require a larger setback.)

2 Mark the fence line with stakes and mason's string. Using a line level as a guide, adjust the string until it is level.

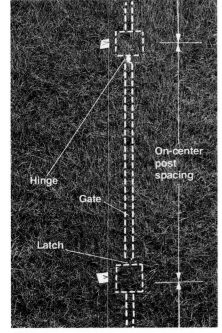

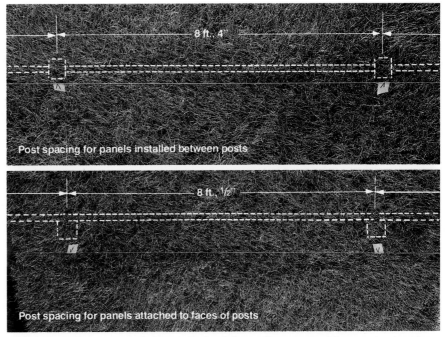

Post spacing for panels installed between posts

Post spacing for panels attached to faces of posts

3 Use masking tape to mark the string where the gate posts will be installed. Measure gate width, including hinges and latch hardware, then add 4" to find the on-center spacing between posts.

4 Mark string at remaining post locations. For a panel fence, try to plan the layout so cut panels will not be needed. If your fence will use 8-ft-long panels installed between 4 × 4 posts, space the posts 8 ft., 4" apart, on-center (top). If panels will be attached to faces of posts, space the posts 8 ft., 1/2" apart, on-center (bottom). For a custom board-and-stringer fence, posts can be set closer together for greater strength.

(continued next page)

5 Use a plumb bob to pinpoint the post locations on the ground, then mark the locations with stakes and remove the string.

6 Dig post holes with a power auger, available at rental centers. Holes should be 6" deeper than the post footing depth specified by your local Building Code. Pour a 6" layer of gravel into each hole to improve drainage.

7 Position each post in its hole. Adjust the post until it is plumb, then brace it with scrap pieces of 2 × 4 driven into the ground and screwed to the sides of the post.

8 When all posts are in position, use the mason's string to make sure the fence line is straight. Adjust the posts, if necessary, until the fence line is straight and the posts are plumb.

9 Fill each post hole with premixed concrete. Overfill the holes slightly. Check posts to make sure they are plumb, then shape the concrete around the bottom of each post to form a rounded crown that will shed water (inset). Let concrete cure for 48 hours before continuing with fence construction.

How to Build a Fence Using Boards & Stringers

1 Install fence posts (pages 61 to 62). Mark cutoff lines on the end posts, 1 ft. below the planned height of the finished fence, than attach a chalk line to the height marks on the end posts, and snap a cutoff line across the posts. (Board-and-stringer fences usually are constructed so the vertical boards extend above the posts.)

2 Trim off the posts along the marked cutoff lines, using a reciprocating saw or handsaw. Brush sealer-preservative onto the cut ends of the posts.

3 Cut 2 × 4 top stringers and coat the ends with sealer-preservative. Center the end joints over the posts, then attach the stringers to the posts with galvanized screws or nails.

4 Mark lines on each post to serve as references for installing additional stringers. Space the marks at 2-ft. intervals.

5 At each stringer reference mark, use galvanized nails to attach a 2" fence bracket to the sides of the posts. Brackets should be flush with the front face of the posts.

(continued next page)

How to Build a Fence Using Boards & Stringers (continued)

6 Position a 2 × 4 stringer between each pair of fence brackets. Hold or tack the stringer against the posts, then mark it for cutting by marking back side along the edges of posts. (If yard is sloped, stringers will be cut at angles.) Cut stringers 1/4" shorter than measurement so stringer will slide into brackets easily.

7 Slide the stringers into the fence brackets and attach them with galvanized nails. If stringers are cut at an angle because of the ground slope, bend the bottom flanges on the fence brackets to match this angle before installing the stringers.

8 Install vertical boards, beginning at an end post. To find board length, measure from the ground to the top edge of the top stringer, then add 10". Cut board to length, then use galvanized screws to attach it to post or rails. Boards should be plumb, and should extend 1 ft. above the top stringer, leaving a 2" gap at the bottom.

9 Measure and cut the remaining fence boards, and attach them to the stringers with galvanized screws. Leave a gap of at least 1/8" between boards (a piece of scrap wood works well as a spacing guide). Each board should extend exactly 1 ft. above the top stringer, and should have a 2" gap at the bottom. At the corners and ends of the fence, you may need to rip-cut fence boards to make them fit.

10 Attach a prebuilt gate, if your project requires one, as shown (page opposite). Finish the fence by coating it with sealer-preservative or paint.

How to Install a Pre-built Gate

1 Attach three evenly spaced hinges to the gate frame, using galvanized screws. Follow the hardware manufacturer's directions, making sure the hinge pins are straight and parallel with the edge of the gate.

2 Position the gate between the gate posts so the hinge pins rest against one post. Set the gate on wood blocks, then attach the hinges to the post with galvanized screws (inset).

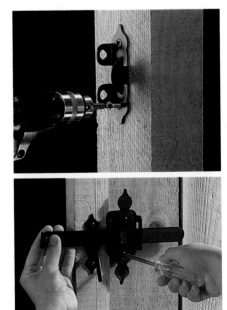

3 Attach the latch hardware to the other gate post and to the gate, using galvanized screws. Open and close the gate to make sure the latch works correctly.

4 Measure and trim the tops of the posts to a uniform height, using a reciprocating saw or handsaw. (If you are not using post caps, cut the posts to a point to help them shed water.)

5 Cover flat post tops with decorative wood or metal caps, and attach them with galvanized casing nails. Coat the fence with sealer-preservative or paint.

Building Garden Ponds

Garden ponds provide a focal point and create a feeling of serenity in any yard. Ponds also expand your planting options and attract new, unusual species of wildlife.

Modern materials have simplified pond-building and made ponds more affordable. Expensive pumps and filtration systems usually are not necessary in small ponds, although they do enable the pond to support more plants and fish.

Artificial garden ponds require pond liners, which are available in two basic types: liner shells and flexible liners. Fiberglass liner shells are easy to install—simply dig a hole and set them in the ground. They are inexpensive and available in many shapes and sizes, but they may crack in very cold weather.

Most garden ponds are built with soft, flexible liners that conform to any shape and size. Some flexible liners are made from polyvinyl chloride (PVC) fabric. PVC liners are economical, but they can become brittle in just a few years.

Better-quality flexible pond liners are made of rubber. Rubber liners are more costly, but also more durable than PVC liners or fiberglass shells.

Everything You Need:

Tools: hose, garden spade, carpenter's level, hand spade or trowel.

Materials: pond liner, sand, mortar mix, flagstone coping stones, long 2 × 4.

Sizing Chart for Flexible Liners		
Liner Size	Maximum Pond Size	
	18" deep	24" deep
8 × 10	4 × 6	3 × 5
10 × 10	6 × 6	5 × 5
10 × 15	6 × 11	5 × 10
15 × 15	11 × 11	10 × 10

Flexible pond liners (above) adapt to nearly any shape or size you want. A shallow shelf holds potted plants. **Fiberglass liner shells** (below) come in many sizes and shapes. Simply set them in the ground and they are ready to stock with fish and aquatic plants.

Photo by Susan Roth

Select a level site for your garden pond. Sloping ground requires a lot of digging and does not provide a natural setting for the pond. Do not build a pond directly under a tree, since fallen leaves contaminate water and root systems make digging difficult. Ponds should not receive too much direct sunshine, however, so choose a site that is in the shadow of a tree or another landscape structure for at least half the day.

Replenish water supply regularly, especially during hot, dry weather. Ponds stocked only with hardy aquatic plants may be replenished with tap water from a garden hose. If the pond is stocked with fish, let water sit for at least three days so chlorine can evaporate before the water is added to the pond.

Collect rainwater in a barrel to replenish ponds that are stocked with fish or very delicate plants. Rainwater is preferable to city water, which contains chemical additives, like chlorine.

(continued next page)

Tips for Building & Maintaining a Garden Pond (continued)

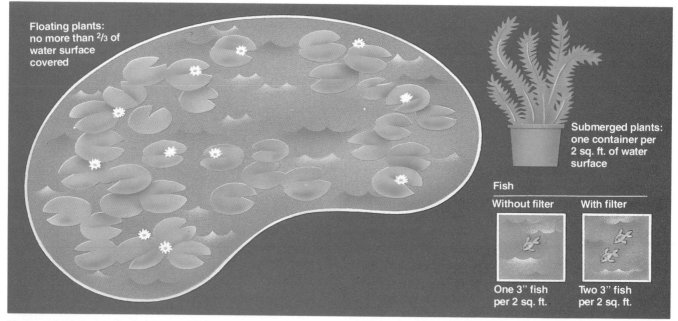

Floating plants: no more than 2/3 of water surface covered

Submerged plants: one container per 2 sq. ft. of water surface

Fish

Without filter	With filter
One 3" fish per 2 sq. ft.	Two 3" fish per 2 sq. ft.

Keep a balance of plants and fish in your pond. Floating plants provide shade for fish and help inhibit algae, but should cover no more than 2/3 of the pond surface. Every pond should have at least one container of submerged plants, which provide oxygen for fish, for every two square feet of pond surface. (NOTE: aquatic plants are available at local nurseries or from mail-order suppliers. Taking aquatic plants from lakes and ponds is illegal in most areas.) Fish add interest to your pond and release carbon dioxide that can be used by plants. Stock no more than one 3" fish per two square feet of surface if your pond does not have an aeration and filtration system. After filling the pond, let water sit for at least one week before stocking it with plants and fish. Ponds with fish should be at least 24" deep.

Planter shown cutaway

Plastic planter

Aquarium gravel

Topsoil

Landscape fabric

1" holes

Build containers for aquatic plants by drilling 1" holes in plastic planters and lining them with landscape fabric. Holes allow water to circulate past the roots of the plants. Planters protect pond liners and simplify maintenance.

Use chemicals sparingly. Little maintenance other than a yearly cleaning is needed for balanced ponds. Water-quality problems, like algae buildup, can be treated with diluted chemical products sold in pet stores.

Bring plants and fish indoors if your pond freezes for more than a week or two during the winter. Cut away plant stems, then store the plants in a dry, dark location. Keep fish in an aerated aquarium during long periods of freezing weather.

How to Install a Garden Pond with a Flexible Liner

1 Select a site for the pond (see page 67) and outline the pond with a hose or heavy rope. Avoid sharp angles, corners, and symmetrical shapes. Ponds should have at least 15 square feet of surface area. Minimum depth is 18" for plants only, and 24" if fish will be added to the pond.

2 Excavate the entire pond area to a depth of about 1 ft. The sides of the pond should slope slightly toward the center. Save some of the topsoil for use with aquatic plants (page opposite).

3 Excavate the center of the pond to maximum depth, plus 2" to allow for a layer of sand. Leave a 1-ft.-wide shelf inside the border to hold aquatic planters. The pond bed should be flat, with walls sloping downward from the shelf.

4 Lay a straight board across the pond, then place a carpenter's level on the board. Check all sides to make sure the edges of the pond are level. If not, adjust the surrounding ground to level by digging, filling, and packing soil. (continued next page)

5 Once the excavation is completed and the site is level, dig a shallow bed around the perimeter of the pond to hold the border flagstones (called coping stones).

6 Remove all stones, roots, and sharp objects from the pond bed, then smooth out the soil base. Next, spread a 2" layer of wet sand on the level areas of the pond bed. Pack the sand with a tamper, then smooth it out with a length of 2 × 4.

OPTION: When using the more inexpensive (and more fragile) PVC pond liners, line the hole with cardboard or old carpeting pieces before installing the liner. The protective layer helps prevent puncturing and stretching of the liner.

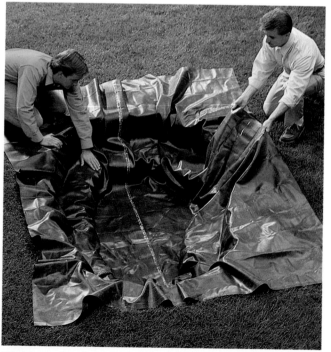

7 Place the liner into the pond bed, then fold and tuck the liner so it conforms to the shape of the hole. Smooth out the liner as much as possible, avoiding any sharp creases.

8 Set a few stones on the overhang to hold the liner in place. Too many stones will cause the liner to stretch, not settle into the hole, when it is filled with water.

9 Fill the pond up to the top with water. Smooth out any large creases or wrinkles that develop as the water level rises. Remove the stones after the pond is full, and allow the liner to settle for one day.

10 Using a scissors, trim the liner so it overhangs the top of the pond by about 12" all the way around the perimeter of the pond.

11 Spread a mixture of 20 parts sand to one part dry mortar in a shallow layer on top of the liner overhang. Spray with a light mist. Set coping stones into the sand so they overhang the edge of the pond by about 2". Set one of the stones ½" lower than the rest, to serve as an overflow point for excess water.

How to Install a Garden Pond with a Liner Shell

1 Set the fiberglass liner shell in place, then use ropes to outline both the flat bottom and the outside edge of the liner on the ground. Use a level to make sure the outline is directly below the outside edge of the shell.

2 Excavate the center of the site to maximum shell depth, then excavate the sides so they slope inward to the flat bottom. Test-fit the shell repeatedly, digging and filling until the shape of the hole matches the shell.

3 Remove all stones and sharp objects, then set the shell into the hole. Check with a level to make sure the shell is level, and adjust the hole as necessary. The top of the shell should be slightly above ground level.

4 Begin slowly filling the shell with water. As the water level rises, pack wet sand into any gaps between the shell and the sides of the hole.

5 Dig a shallow bed around the perimeter of the liner to hold coping stones, if desired. Place the stones near the pond liner, but do not set them on the liner edges. Any weight on the edges of fiberglass shell could cause it to crack.

Building Decks

Deck Planning

Parts of a Deck

Structural parts of a deck include posts, beams, ledgers, and joists. They support and distribute the weight of the deck. For economy and durability, use pressure-treated lumber for these parts. The other parts of a deck include the decking, facing, railings, and stairway. Use redwood or cedar for these visible parts.

Ledgers anchor an attached deck to a house. Ledgers support one end of all joists.

Concrete footings with post anchors support the weight of the deck and hold the deck posts in place. They are made by pouring concrete into tube forms. Local climates and building codes determine depth of footings. **Post anchors** should be made of galvanized steel to resist corrosion.

Posts transfer the weight of the deck to the footings. They are attached to the post anchors with galvanized nails, and to the beam with lag screws.

Beams provide the main structural support for the deck. A beam is usually made from a pair of 2 × 8s or 2 × 10s attached to the deck posts.

Joists support the decking. For an attached deck, the joists are fastened at one end to the **ledger** and at the other end to the **header joist**. The **outside joists** can be covered with redwood or cedar **facing** boards for appearance.

Decking is the main feature of any deck. The decking boards are attached to the joists with galvanized screws or nails.

Railing parts include **railing posts** and **balusters** attached to the header and outside joists, a horizontal **rail**, and a **cap**. Building codes may require railings on decks 24" or more above ground level, and fully graspable handrails on stairways.

A stairway is made from a pair of **stringers** fastened to the side of the deck, and a series of **treads** attached to the stringers with metal cleats.

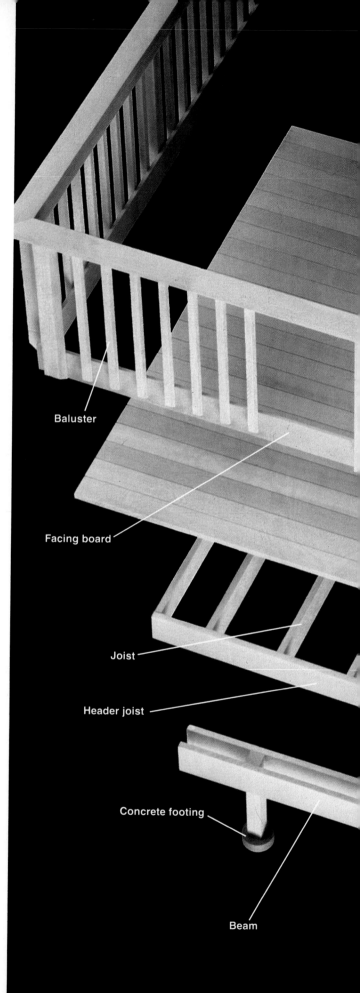

Baluster

Facing board

Joist

Header joist

Concrete footing

Beam

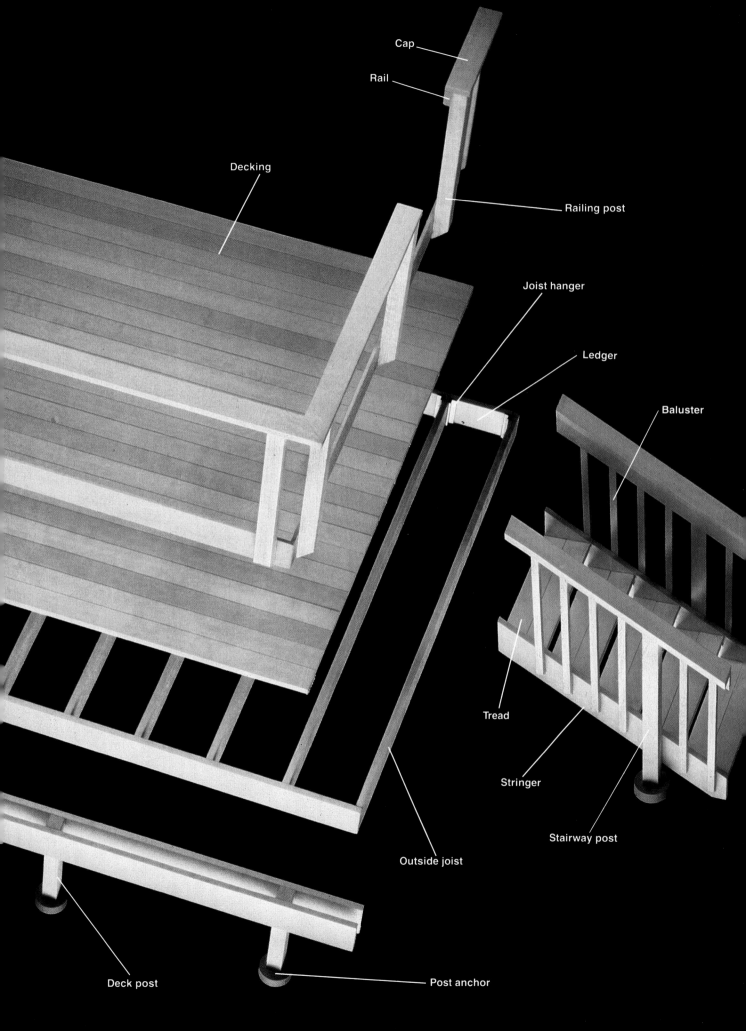

Cap

Rail

Decking

Railing post

Joist hanger

Ledger

Baluster

Tread

Stringer

Outside joist

Stairway post

Deck post

Post anchor

Pressure-treated Lumber

Pressure-treated lumber is the strongest and least expensive choice for deck lumber. Pressure-treated lumber resists rot and insects and is an excellent building material for outdoor use.

Treated lumber is created by forcing chemical preservatives into it under high pressure. The most common treatment uses chromated copper arsenate, identified by the label "CCA." The preservative usually gives the wood a green color, which fades with time. Or, you can stain pressure-treated wood in a variety of colors.

Pressure-treated lumber is rated by the amount of chemical retained by the wood. For decks, choose lumber with a retention level of .40, approved for direct ground contact. This is sometimes signified by the code "LP 22" stamped on the wood.

Pressure-treated lumber can be used to build the entire deck; or, it can be used only for posts, beams, and joists, with redwood or cedar used for decking, stairways, facing, and railings.

Caution:
The chemicals in pressure-treated lumber are toxic. Wear eye protection, a particle mask, and long sleeves and pants to avoid contact with sawdust from pressure-treated wood.

Grade stamp for pressure-treated lumber lists the type of preservative used and the chemical retention level of the wood. Look for "CCA" label indicating that chromated copper arsenate is the preservative. Make sure lumber carries the label "LP 22," or ".40 retention." Other information found on grade stamp includes proper exposure rating, and name and location of treating company.

Redwood

Redwood is an attractive wood often used for outdoor structures. The heartwood has a brownish red color and is naturally resistant to decay. The cream-colored sapwood should be treated with wood preservative when used in a deck.

Quality redwood is somewhat expensive, so it is often used only for visible parts of the deck, like decking and railings.

Redwood is available in more than 30 grades. "Construction heart" or "merchantable heart" are medium-quality grades that are good choices for a deck.

Cedar

The cedar species recommended for decks include red cedar and incense cedar. Cedar has a light brown appearance, with an attractive grain. Because it ages to a uniform silver-gray, cedar is often used where a weathered appearance is desired.

Heartwood cedar is naturally resistant to decay. Sapwood cedar is white or cream-colored, and should be treated with wood preservative when used in a deck.

Cedar can be used for the visible surfaces of the deck. For structural members like joists, beams, and posts, use pressure-treated lumber.

Grade stamp for redwood lists wood dryness, lumber grade, and membership association. Redwood should be certified "KILN DRIED" or "DRY"; and graded as clear redwood (CLR RWD), construction heartwood (CONST HT), merchantable heartwood (MERCH HT), or construction redwood (CONST RWD).

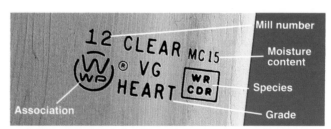

Grade stamp for cedar lists the lumber mill number, the moisture content, the species, the lumber grade, and membership association. Western red cedar (WRC) or incense cedar (INC) used in decks should be graded as heartwood (HEART) with a maximum moisture content of 15% (MC 15).

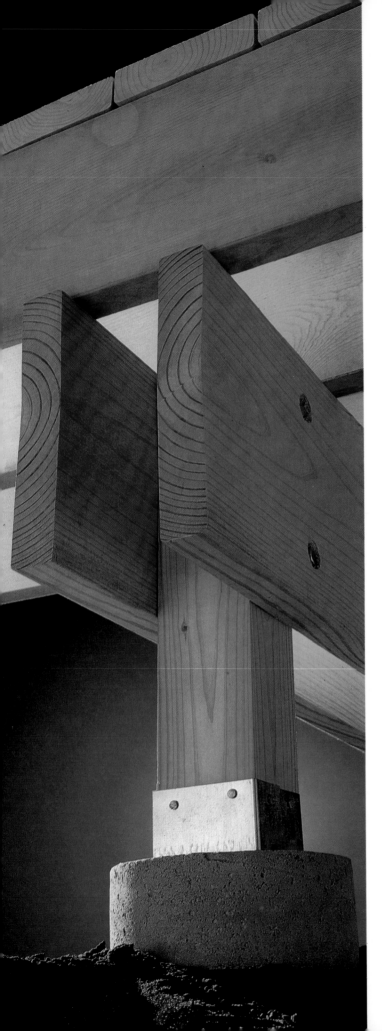

Lumber Size & Deck Planning

A deck has seven major structural parts: the **ledger, decking, joists,** one or more **beams, posts, stairway stringers,** and **stairway treads.** To create a working design plan, you must know the span limits of each part of the deck. The ledger is attached directly to the house and does not have a span limit.

A span limit is the safe distance a board can cross without support from underneath. The maximum safe span depends on the size of the board. For example, 2×6 joists spaced 16" on-center can safely span 9' 9", while 2×10 joists can span 16' 5".

Begin planning by first choosing size and pattern of the decking. Then determine the size and layout of the joists, beams, and posts, using the span tables on the opposite page. In general, a deck designed with larger-size lumber, like 2×12 joists and beams, requires fewer pieces, because the boards have a large span limit.

Nominal	Actual
1×4	$\frac{3}{4}$" $\times$ $3\frac{3}{4}$"
1×6	$\frac{3}{4}$" $\times$ $5\frac{3}{4}$"
2×4	$1\frac{1}{2}$" $\times$ $3\frac{1}{2}$"
2×6	$1\frac{1}{2}$" $\times$ $5\frac{1}{2}$"
2×8	$1\frac{1}{2}$" $\times$ $7\frac{1}{4}$"
2×10	$1\frac{1}{2}$" $\times$ $9\frac{1}{4}$"
2×12	$1\frac{1}{2}$" $\times$ $11\frac{1}{4}$"
4×4	$3\frac{1}{2}$" $\times$ $3\frac{1}{2}$"
6×6	$5\frac{1}{2}$" $\times$ $5\frac{1}{2}$"

Nominal vs. Actual Lumber Dimensions: When planning a deck, remember that the actual size of lumber is smaller than the nominal size by which lumber is sold. Use the actual dimensions when drawing a deck design plan.

Span Limit Tables for Deck Lumber

Recommended Decking Span Between Joists:
Decking boards can be made from a variety of lumber sizes. For a basic deck use 2 × 4 or 2 × 6 lumber with joists spaced 16" apart.

Decking Boards	Recommended Span
1 × 4 or 1 × 6, laid straight	16"
1 × 4 or 1 × 6, laid diagonal	12"
2 × 4 or 2 × 6, laid straight	16"
2 × 4 or 2 × 6, laid diagonal	12"
2 × 4, laid on edge	24"

Maximum Joist Span Between Supports: Maximum joist span between supports depends on the size of the joists and the spacing between joists. For example, a deck with 2 × 8 joists spaced 16" apart requires supports no more than 12' 10" apart. On a cantilevered deck, the joists may extend past the beam by a distance equal to one-third the total length of the joists.

Joist Size	Joist Spacing (on center)		
	12"	16"	24"
2 × 6	11' 7"	9' 9"	7' 11"
2 × 8	15' 0"	12' 10"	10' 6"
2 × 10	19' 6"	16' 5"	13' 4"

Maximum Beam Span Between Posts: Maximum beam span depends on the size of the beams and their spacing. For example, a deck with a 4 × 8 beam, and joists that span 12 feet should have posts that are no more than 7 feet apart.

Beam Size	Joist Span			
	6 ft.	8 ft.	10 ft.	12 ft.
4 × 6 (two 2 × 6s)	8 ft.	7 ft.	6 ft.	5 ft.
4 × 8 (two 2 × 8s)	10 ft.	9 ft.	8 ft.	7 ft.
4 × 10 (two 2 × 10s)	12 ft.	11 ft.	10 ft.	9 ft.
4 × 12 (two 2 × 12s)	14 ft.	13 ft.	12 ft.	11 ft.

Recommended Post Size: Choose post size by finding the load area for the deck. To find the load area, multiply the distance between beams by the distance between posts. For example, on a deck that has one beam spaced 10 feet from the ledger, with posts spaced 7 feet apart, the load area is 70. If this deck is less than 6 feet high, the recommended post size is 4 × 4.

Deck Height	Load Area — Multiply distance between beams (feet) times the distance between posts (feet).				
	48	72	96	120	144
Up to 6 ft.	4 × 4	4 × 4	6 × 6	6 × 6	6 × 6
More than 6 ft.	6 × 6	6 × 6	6 × 6	6 × 6	6 × 6

Minimum Stair Stringer Sizes: Size of stair stringers depends on the span of the stairway. For example, if the bottom of the stairway lies 7 feet from the deck, build the stringers from 2 × 12s.

Span of Stairway	Stringer Size
Up to 6 ft.	2 × 10
More than 6 ft.	2 × 12

Recommended Railing Sizes: Size of posts, rails, and caps depends on the spacing of the railing posts. For example, if railing posts are spaced 6 feet apart, use 4 × 4 posts and 2 × 6 rails and caps.

Space Between Railing Posts	Post Size	Cap Size	Rail Size
2 ft. to 3 ft.	2 × 4	2 × 4	2 × 4
3 ft. to 4 ft.	4 × 4	2 × 4	2 × 4
4 ft. to 6 ft.	4 × 4	2 × 6	2 × 6

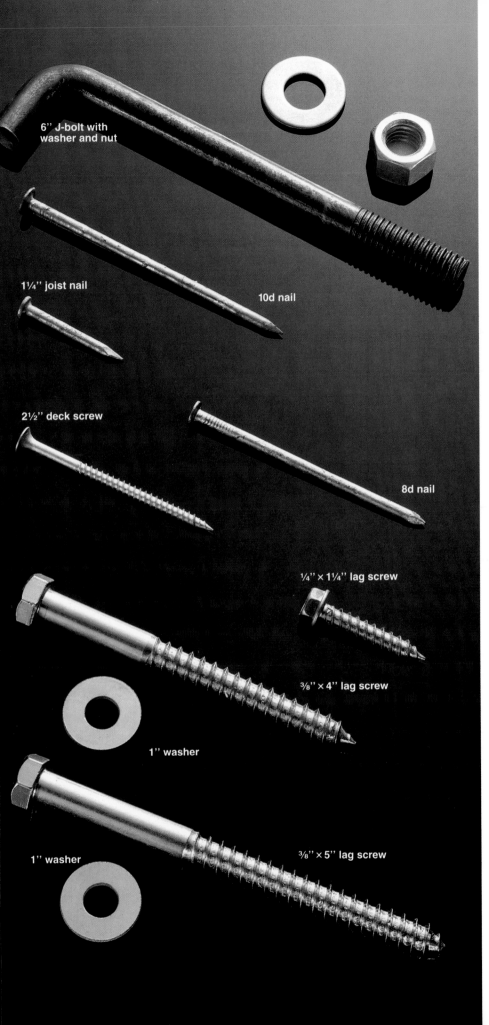

6" J-bolt with washer and nut

1¼" joist nail

10d nail

2½" deck screw

8d nail

¼" × 1¼" lag screw

⅜" × 4" lag screw

1" washer

1" washer

⅜" × 5" lag screw

Hardware & Fasteners

Build your deck with galvanized lumber connectors, nails, and screws. Galvanized metal products resist rust and will not stain the wood.

Metal lumber connectors are used to create strong joints with wood framing members. Post anchors, joist hangers, and brackets are available at lumberyards and home improvement centers.

Seal heads of counterbored screws with silicone caulk to prevent water damage.

Hot-dipped galvanized nails (above) have a thick zinc coating and rough surface. Hot-dipped nails will not rust or stain wood.

Deck fasteners (left), include 6" J-bolt with nut and washer, 8d and 10d galvanized nails, 1¼" galvanized joist nail, 2½" corrosion-resistant deck screw, ¼" × 1¼" lag screw, ⅜" × 4" lag screw, ⅜" × 5" lag screw, and 1" washer.

Flashing fits over ledger to protect wood from moisture damage. Top edge of flashing tucks up under the siding.

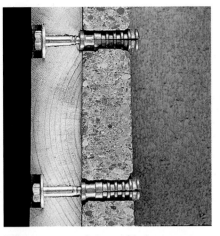

Masonry anchors with lag screws hold the ledger to stone, brick, or concrete blocks.

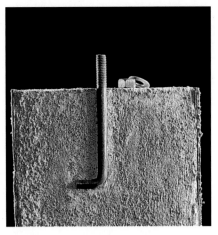

J-bolts with nuts and washers hold the post anchors to the concrete footings.

Post anchors hold deck posts in place, and raise the base of the posts to help prevent water from entering end grain of wood.

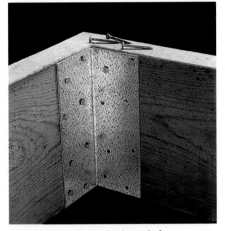

Angle brackets help reinforce header and outside joists. Angle brackets are also used to attach stair stringers to the deck.

Joist hangers are used to attach joists to the ledger and header joist. Double hanger is used when decking pattern requires a double-width joist.

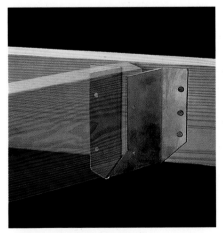

Angled joist hangers are used to frame decks that have unusual angles or decking patterns.

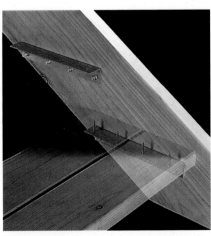

Stair cleats support the treads of deck steps. Cleats are attached to stair stringers with ¼'' × 1¼'' galvanized lag screws.

Silicone caulk seals lag screw heads and any cracks that may trap water. Choose an exterior-grade caulk rated for lifetime use.

Concrete

Use concrete to make solid footings that will support the weight of the deck. Concrete for footings is made from a mixture of portland cement, sand, and coarse gravel (¼" to 1½" in diameter). These materials can be purchased separately and mixed at home, or you can buy bags containing the pre-mixed dry ingredients. For larger amounts, buy ready-mixed concrete in trailer loads.

For most deck projects, mixing your own concrete is easy and inexpensive. Mix concrete in a wheelbarrow or with a power mixer, available at tool rental centers.

The estimation charts on the opposite page give approximate volumes of concrete. You may have a small amount of concrete left over after pouring post footings.

Mix concrete ingredients in a wheelbarrow. Use a ratio of 1 part portland cement (A), 2 parts sand (B), and 3 parts coarse gravel (C). Or, use the cubic-foot volumes shown in the chart (page opposite).

Amount of Concrete Needed (cubic feet)

Number of 8" Diameter Footings	Depth of Footings (feet)			
	1	2	3	4
2	¾	1½	2¼	3
3	1	2¼	3½	4½
4	1½	3	4½	6
5	2	3¾	5¾	7½

Concrete Ingredient Amounts

Amount of Concrete Needed (cubic feet)	Dry Ingredients for Self-mix			60-lb. bags of premixed dry concrete
	94-lb. bags of portland cement	Cubic feet of sand	Cubic feet of gravel	
1	⅙	⅓	½	2
2	⅓	⅔	1	4
3	½	1½	3	6
4	¾	1¾	3½	8
5	1	2¼	4½	10
10	2	4½	9	20

Buying & Mixing Concrete

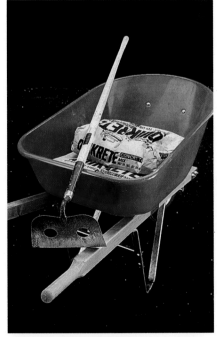

Buy premixed bags of dry concrete for small jobs. A 60-lb. bag creates about ½ of a cubic foot of concrete. A 90-lb. bag creates about ⅔ of a cubic foot.

Rent a power cement mixer to blend large amounts of cement, gravel, sand, and water quickly.

Buy ready-mixed concrete for larger jobs. Trailer loads are available at rental centers, and are sold by the cubic yard. One cubic yard equals 27 cubic feet.

Ratchet wrench & socket

Shovel

Trowel

32-oz. masonry hammer

22-oz. claw hammer

Metal snips

Cat's paw

50-ft. tape measure

16-ft. tape measure

Caulk gun

Hoe

Rubber mallet

Clamshell posthole digger

Combination square

Mason's string

Compass

Plumb bob

Flat pry bar

Line level

Scratch awl

Torpedo level

Chalk line

1"chisel

Putty knife

Level

Framing square

Hand tools for deck building should have heavy-duty construction. Metal tools should be made from high-carbon steel with smoothly finished surfaces. Buy quality hand tools that are well balanced, and that have tight, comfortably molded handles. There is no substitute for quality.

Tool Basics

With a set of basic hand and power tools, you can complete any of the deck projects shown in this book. You may already own many of the tools needed. If you buy new tools, invest in quality, heavy-duty products that will provide long service.

Some specialty tools, like power miter boxes or reciprocating saws, are available at tool rental centers. Or, they can be purchased at home improvement stores.

Always wear eye protection when using tools. Always wear a particle mask and work gloves when sawing or handling pressure-treated lumber, because the chemicals in the wood are toxic.

Tools for finishing and maintaining a deck include: rubber gloves (A), shop vacuum (B), 14-gauge extension cord (C), pressure sprayer (D), hydraulic jack and handle (E), eye protection (F), scrub brush (G), paint brush (H), particle mask (I), and orbital sander (J).

Power tools include: power miter box (A), circular saw (B) with carbide-tipped blade and Teflon®-coated carbide blade, reciprocating saw (C), ³⁄₈" drill and bits (D), jig saw (E), and screwgun (F). These tools should have heavy-duty motors. Screwgun is designed for driving long deck screws through 2" lumber. Reciprocating saw and power miter box can be purchased at home centers, or leased at tool rental outlets.

Make a map of the features of your house and yard. Include any features that might affect how you build and use your deck, like sun and shade patterns, trees, and other landscaping details. For accurate measurements, use a long tape measure and hold it level and perpendicular to the house.

Creating Site Drawings

Create site drawings of the building area before designing a deck. Show all details that may affect how you build and use the deck.

Building a deck requires two types of site drawings. A **plan view** shows the building site as viewed from directly overhead. An **elevation** shows the vertical details of the site as it is viewed from the side or front.

As you create site drawings, consider how the features of house and yard influence the deck design. Remember that the building site is affected by weather, time of day, and seasonal changes.

For example, if your deck will be used mainly for summertime evening meals, look at the sun, shade, and wind patterns on the site during this time of day.

Everything You Need:

Tools: pencil or marker, eraser, 50-ft. tape measure, ruler, compass, line level.

Materials: large sheets of paper.

Supplies: mason's string.

How to Create Plan-view Site Drawings

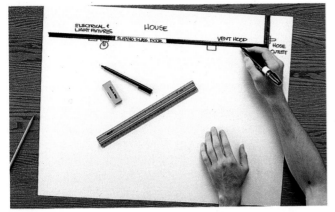

1 Sketch position of house and yard on a large sheet of paper, using a scale of 1'' equals 1 foot. Show position of doors, windows, and outdoor utilities, like garden hose spigots, or light fixtures.

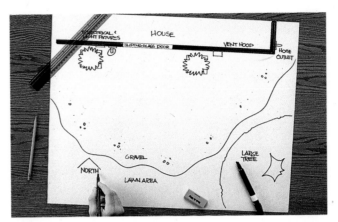

2 Add a symbol to the site drawing to indicate north. Mark the location of trees, gardening beds or planters, and any other landscaping features. Show any overhead or underground utility lines.

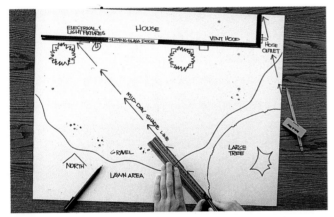

3 Observe the deck site during the time of day when the deck will be used most often. Outline shade and sun patterns on the site drawing.

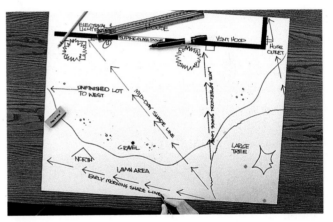

4 Show how the site changes throughout the day. Outline shade and sun patterns at different times, and quality of nearby view. Note changes in winds, traffic noise, and neighborhood activity.

How to Create Elevation Site Drawings

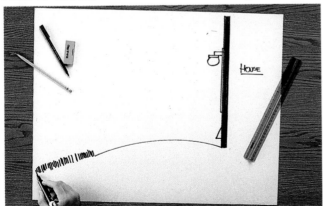

1 Create a side-view elevation map of your site, showing the slope of the ground and the position of the house. For accuracy, stretch level mason's strings from the house, and use the strings for reference to determine slope of ground.

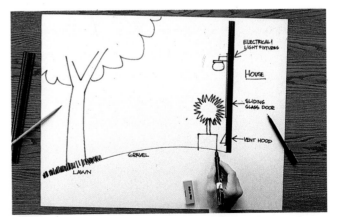

2 Add any other features that will affect how you build and use the deck, like the height of tree branches or telephone wires, shrubs, flowerbeds, or other landscaping details.

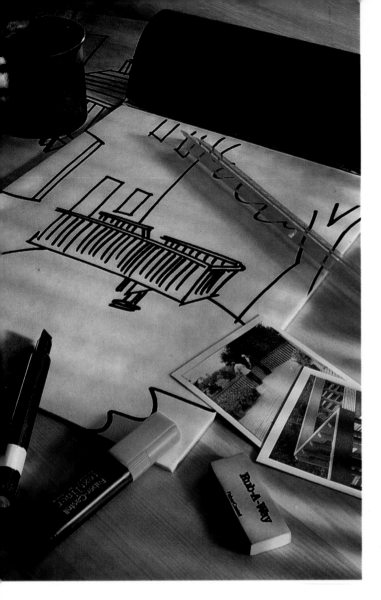

Drawing Design Plans

Design plans help you estimate lumber and hardware needs, and provide the measurements needed to lay out the deck and cut the lumber. If a work permit is required by local codes, you must have design plans.

You will need two types of design drawings for a deck project. A **plan view** shows the parts of the deck as they are viewed from directly overhead. An **elevation** shows the deck parts as viewed from the side or front.

To avoid confusion, do not try to show all parts of the deck in a single plan view. First, draw one plan that shows the outline of the deck and the pattern of the decking boards. Then make another plan that shows the underlying ledger, joists, beams, and posts.

Everything You Need:

Tools: pencil or marker, eraser, ruler.

Materials: site drawing, large sheets of paper, sheets of tissue paper.

How to Draw Design Plans

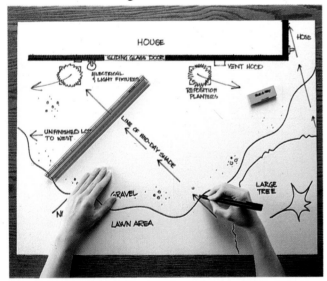

1 Use the scaled site drawings (pages 86 to 87) to help establish the size and shape of the deck.

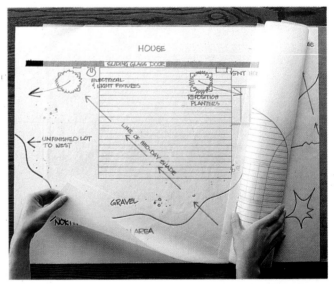

2 Lay a sheet of tissue paper over the site drawing and tape in position. Experiment with deck ideas by sketching different designs on separate sheets of tissue paper.

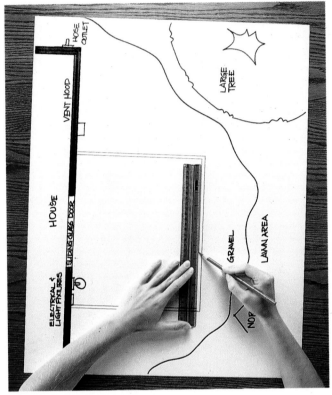

3 Make copies of the scaled site drawing. Use a ruler and sharp pencil to draw the outline of the deck on one copy of the scaled site drawing.

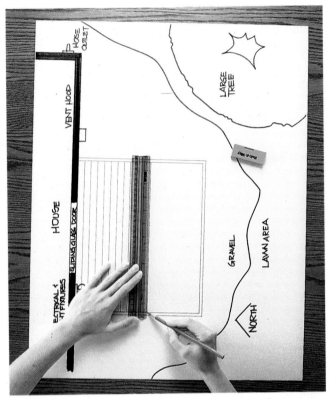

4 Draw in the decking pattern over the outline. Indicate the size and type of lumber and hardware to be used. Save this plan for reference.

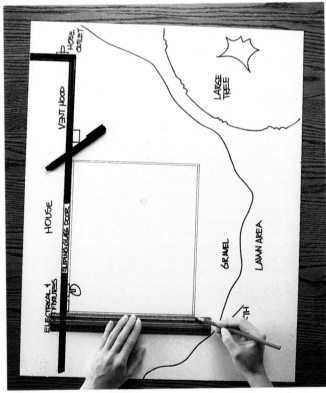

5 On a second copy of the scaled site drawing, draw another outline of the deck. Draw in the ledger, the outside joists, and the header joist.

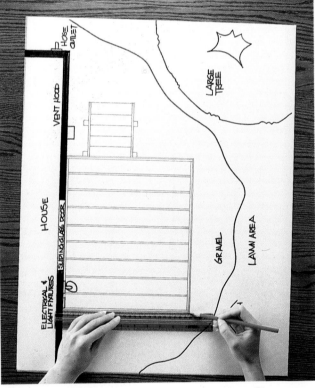

6 Draw the inner joists, and any blocking. Show any facing boards that will be used. Show the stairway stringers, treads, and posts.

(continued next page)

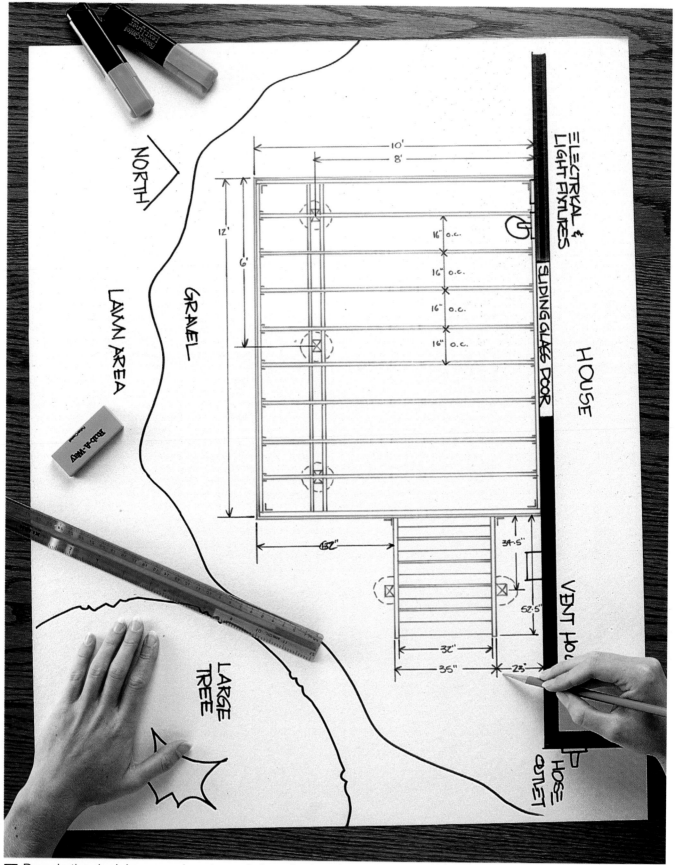

7 Draw in the deck beam and posts, and show the location of the concrete footings. List all deck dimensions on the plan. Save this drawing for reference when ordering lumber and hardware.

How to Draw Design Elevations

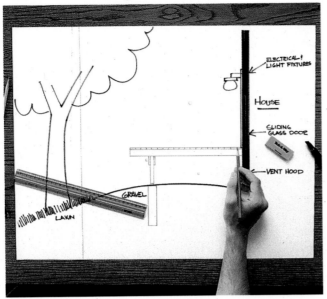

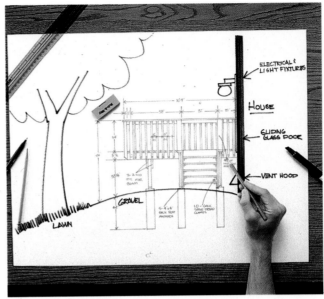

1 Draw in the basic deck platform on the site elevation drawing (page 87). Draw in the beam and the posts.

2 Add the stairway to the elevation drawing, then draw in the railing posts, balusters, rails and caps. List all dimensions on the drawing, and indicate size, type, and quantities of lumber and hardware needed. Save this drawing for reference.

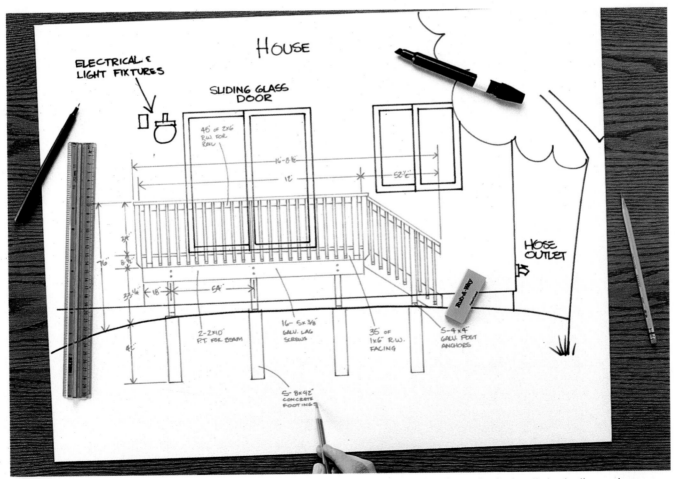

3 Create another design elevation showing the deck as viewed from the front. Include all deck dimensions, and indicate the size and type of lumber and hardware to be used. Save this drawing for reference.

Ordering Lumber & Materials

Use the deck design plans and elevations to help make a complete list of the items you will need. For convenience, copy the checklist on the opposite page. Add 10% to lumber and material estimates to compensate for flaws in materials and construction errors.

Most supplies for building a deck are available at lumberyards or home improvement centers. Full-service lumberyards have a complete selection of building materials, but prices may be higher than those at home improvement centers. The quality of lumber at home centers can vary, so inspect the wood and hand-pick the pieces you want.

Order top-quality hardware, caulks, wood sealers, and stains. Save money on nails, screws, and other hardware by buying them in large quantities.

Buy top-quality products for a long-lasting deck, including: alkyd-based sealers and stains (A, B, C), galvanized post anchors (D), galvanized nails (E), galvanized joist hangers (F), corrosion-resistant deck screws (G), silicone caulk (H).

Lumber & Materials Checklist

Item	Size, type	Quantity	Where to buy	Price each	Total price
Lumber					
Ledger					
Posts					
Beams					
Joists					
Decking					
Stair stringers					
Stair treads					
Railing posts					
Balusters or rails					
Hardware					
Flashing					
Galvanized nails					
1¼" joist nails					
Post anchors					
Lag screws					
Deck screws					
Joist hangers					
Joist angle brackets					
Metal stair cleats					
Concrete					
Concrete forms					
Portland cement					
Sand					
Gravel					
Miscellaneous					
Silicone caulk					
Sealer/stain					
Equipment rental					
Tools to buy					

Photocopy this checklist for reference when ordering lumber and materials.

Building Decks:
A Step-by-Step Overview

Review the design plan (pages 88 to 91) and the directions on pages 96 to 143 before beginning deck construction. Build the deck in several stages, and gather tools and materials for each stage before beginning. Arrange to have a helper for the more difficult stages.

Check with local utilities for the location of underground electrical, telephone, or water lines. Apply for a building permit, where required, and make sure a building inspector has approved the deck design before beginning work.

The time it takes to build a deck depends on the size and complexity of the design. A rectangular deck, about 10 ft. × 14 ft., can be completed in two or three weekends.

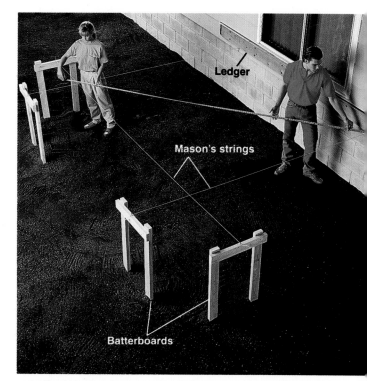

1 Install a ledger to anchor the deck to the house and to serve as reference for laying out footings (pages 96 to 101). Use batterboards and mason's strings to locate footings, and check for square by measuring diagonals (pages 102 to 107).

4 Install metal joist hangers on the ledger and header joist, then hang the remaining joists (pages 123 to 126). Most decking patterns require joists that are spaced 16" on center.

5 Lay decking boards, and trim them with a circular saw (pages 127 to 129). If desired for appearance, cover pressure-treated header and outside joists with redwood or cedar facing boards (page 129).

2 Pour concrete post footings (pages 108 to 111), and install metal post anchors (pages 113 to 114). Set and brace the posts, attach them to the post anchors, and mark posts to show where beam will be attached (pages 114 to 117).

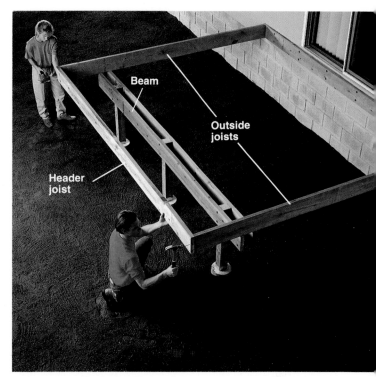

Beam

Outside joists

Header joist

3 Attach the beam to the posts (pages 118 to 121). Install the outside joists and header joist, using galvanized nails (pages 122 to 123).

6 Build deck stairs (pages 130 to 135). Stairs provide access to the deck and establish traffic patterns.

7 Install a railing around the deck and stairway (pages 136 to 143). A railing adds a decorative touch, and may be required on any deck that is more than 24" above the ground.

Installing a Ledger

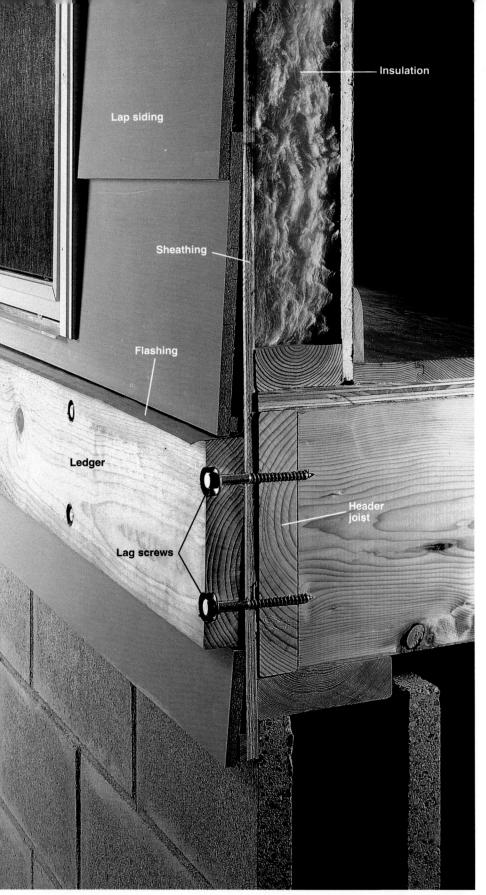

The first step in building an attached deck is to fasten the ledger to the house. The ledger anchors the deck and establishes a reference point for building the deck square and level. The ledger also supports one end of all the deck joists, so it must be attached securely to the framing members of the house.

Install the ledger so that the surface of the decking boards will be 1" below the indoor floor level. This height difference prevents rainwater or melted snow from seeping into the house.

Some people prefer to install the ledger using standoff brackets. These brackets attach to the header joist and the ledger is then connected to them, creating a gap between the ledger and the house which helps prevent moisture damage to the wood. Standoff brackets can be found at home building centers. If you use brackets, follow the manufacturer's instructions for installing the ledger; our instructions do not use standoff brackets to do this.

Everything You Need:

Tools (page 84): pencil, level, circular saw with carbide blade, chisel, hammer, metal snips, caulk gun, drill and bits (1/4" twist, 1" spade, 3/8" and 5/8" masonry), ratchet wrench, awl, rubber mallet.

Materials: pressure-treated lumber, galvanized flashing, 8d galvanized common nails, silicone caulk, 3/8" × 4" lag screws and 1" washers, lead masonry anchors for 3/8" lag screws (for brick walls).

Supplies: 2 × 4s for braces.

Ledger (shown in cross section) is made from pressure-treated lumber. Lap siding is cut away to expose sheathing and to provide a flat surface for attaching the ledger. Galvanized flashing tucked under siding prevents moisture damage to wood. Countersunk 3/8" × 4" lag screws hold ledger to header joist inside house.

How to Attach a Ledger to Lap Siding

1 Draw an outline showing where the deck will fit against the house, using a level as a guide. Include the thickness of the outside joists and any decorative facing boards that will be installed.

2 Cut out siding along outline, using a circular saw. Set blade depth to same thickness as siding, so that blade does not cut into sheathing.

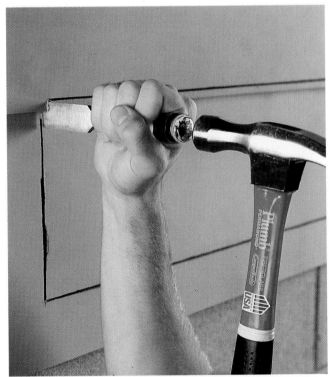

3 Use a chisel to finish the cutout where circular saw blade does not reach. Hold the chisel with the bevel-side in.

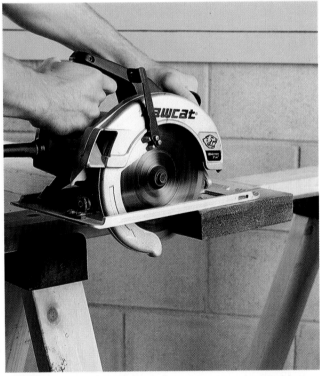

4 Measure and cut ledger from pressure-treated lumber. Remember that ledger will be shorter than overall length of cutout.

(continued next page)

5 Cut galvanized flashing to length of cutout, using metal snips. Slide flashing up under siding.

6 Center the ledger in the cutout, underneath the flashing. Brace in position, and tack ledger into place with 8d galvanized nails. Apply a thick bead of silicone caulk to crack between siding and flashing.

7 Drill pairs of ¼" pilot holes spaced every 2 feet, through the ledger and sheathing and into the header joist.

8 Counterbore each pilot hole to ½" depth, using a 1" spade bit.

9 Attach ledger to wall with ⅜" × 4" lag screws and washers, using a ratchet wrench.

10 Seal lag screw heads with silicone caulk. Seal the crack between the wall and the sides and bottom of the ledger.

How to Attach a Ledger to Masonry

1 Measure and cut ledger. Ledger will be shorter than overall length of cutout. Drill pairs of ¼" pilot holes every 2 feet in ledger. Counterbore each pilot hole to ½" depth, using a 1" spade bit.

2 Draw an outline of the deck on the wall, using a level as a guide. Center ledger in outline on wall, and brace in position. Mark the pilot hole locations on wall, using an awl or nail. Remove ledger.

(continued next page)

How to Attach a Ledger to Masonry (continued)

3 Drill anchor holes 3" deep into masonry, using a ⅝" masonry bit.

4 Drive lead masonry anchors for ⅜" lag screws into drilled holes, using a rubber mallet.

5 Attach ledger to wall with ⅜" × 4" lag screws and washers, using a ratchet wrench. Tighten screws firmly, but do not overtighten.

6 Seal the cracks between the wall and ledger with silicone caulk. Also seal the lag screw heads.

How to Attach a Ledger to Stucco

1 Draw outline of deck on wall, using a level as a guide. Measure and cut ledger, and drill pilot holes (page 99, step 1). Brace ledger against wall, and mark hole locations, using a nail or awl.

2 Remove ledger. Drill pilot holes through stucco layer of wall, using a ⅜" masonry bit.

3 Extend each pilot hole through the sheathing and into the header joist, using a ¼" bit. Reposition ledger and brace in place.

4 Attach ledger to wall with ⅜" × 4" lag screws and washers, using a ratchet wrench. Seal the lag screw heads and the cracks between the wall and ledger with silicone caulk.

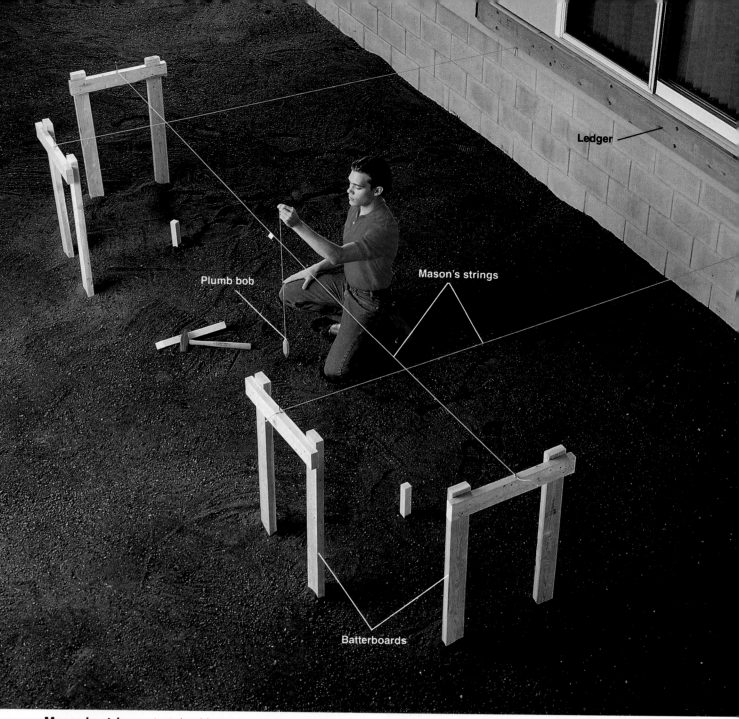

Mason's strings stretched between ledger and batterboards are used to position footings for deck posts. Use a plumb bob and stakes to mark the ground at the exact centerpoints of footings.

Locating Post Footings

Establish the exact locations of all concrete footings by stretching mason's strings across the site. Use the ledger board as a starting point. These perpendicular layout strings will be used to locate holes for concrete footings, and to position metal post anchors on the finished footings. Anchor the layout strings with temporary 2 × 4 supports, often called batterboards.

Everything You Need:

Tools: tape measure, felt-tipped pen, circular saw, screwgun, framing square, masonry hammer, claw hammer, line level, plumb bob.

Supplies: 2 × 4s, 10d nails, 2½" wallboard screws, mason's strings, masking tape.

How to Locate Post Footings

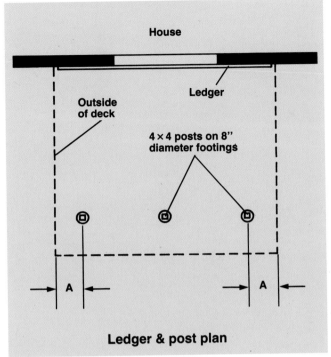

House

Ledger

Outside of deck

4 × 4 posts on 8" diameter footings

A ← → A ← →

Ledger & post plan

1 Use the design plan (page 90) to find distance (A). Measure from the side of the deck to the center of each outside post. Use the elevation drawings (page 91) to find the height of each deck post.

2 Cut 2 × 4 stakes for batterboards, each about 8" longer than post height. Trim one end of each stake to a point, using a circular saw. Cut 2 × 4 crosspieces, each about 2 feet long.

3 Assemble batterboards by attaching crosspieces to stakes with 2½" wallboard screws. Crosspieces should be about 2" below tops of stakes.

4 Transfer measurement A (step 1) to ledger, and mark reference points at each end of ledger. String lines will be stretched from these points on ledger. When measuring, remember to allow for outside joists and facing that will be butted to the ends of the ledger.

(continued next page)

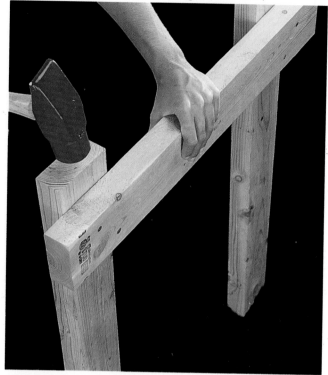

5 Drive a batterboard 6" into the ground, about 2 feet past the post location. Crosspiece of batterboard should be parallel to the ledger.

6 Drive a 10d nail into bottom of ledger at reference point (step 4). Attach a mason's string to nail.

7 Extend the mason's string so that it is taut and perpendicular to the ledger. Use a framing square as a guide. Secure the string temporarily by wrapping it several times around the batterboard.

8 Check the mason's string for square using "3-4-5 carpenter's triangle." First, measure along the ledger 3 feet from the mason's string and mark a point, using a felt-tipped pen.

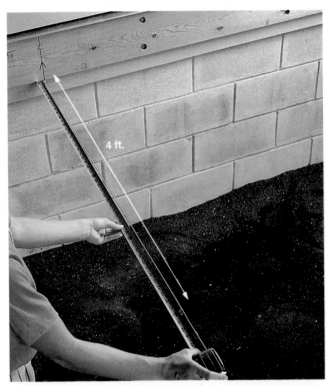

9 Measure mason's string 4 feet from edge of ledger, and mark with masking tape.

10 Measure distance between marks. If string is perpendicular to ledger, the distance will be exactly 5 feet. If necessary, move string left or right on batterboard until distance between marks is 5 feet.

11 Drive a 10d nail into top of batterboard at string location. Leave about 2" of nail exposed. Tie string to nail.

(continued next page)

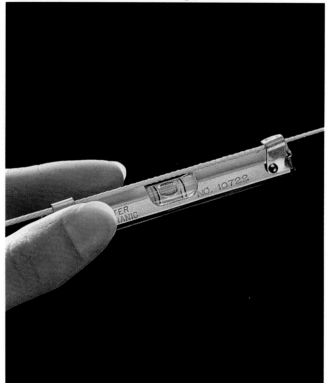

12 Hang a line level on the mason's string. Raise or lower string until it is level. Locate other outside post footing, repeating steps 5 to 12.

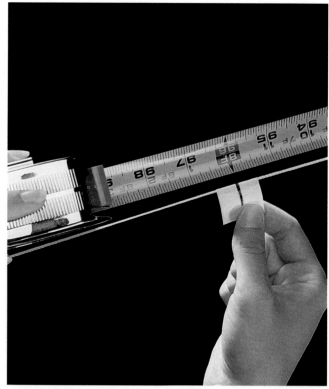

13 Measure along mason's strings from ledger to find centerpoint of posts. Mark centerpoints on strings, using masking tape.

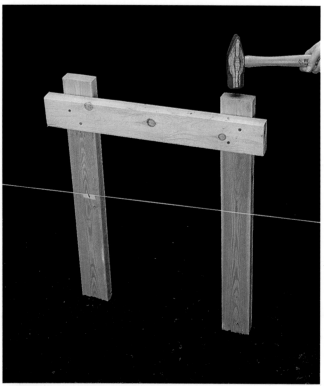

14 Drive additional batterboards into ground, about 2 feet outside mason's strings and lined up with post centerpoint marks (step 13).

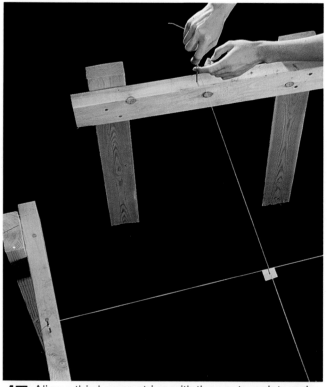

15 Align a third cross string with the centerpoint marks on the first strings. Drive 10d nails in new batterboards, and tie off cross string on nails. Cross string should be close to, but not touching, the first strings.

Cross string

16 Check strings for square by measuring distances A-B and C-D. Measure diagonals A-D and B-C from edge of ledger to opposite corners. If strings are square, measurement A-B will be same as C-D, and diagonal A-D will be same as B-C. If necessary, adjust strings on batterboards until square.

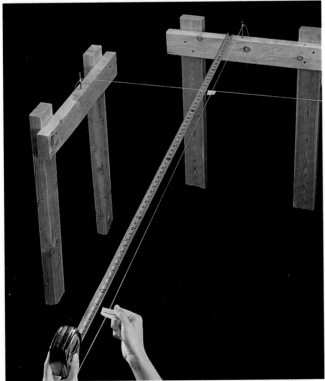

17 Measure along the cross string and mark centerpoints of any posts that will be installed between the outside posts.

18 Use a plumb bob to mark post centerpoints on the ground, directly under the marks on the mason's strings. Drive a stake into ground at each point. Remove mason's strings before digging footings.

Digging & Pouring Footings

Power augers quickly dig holes for post footings. They are available at rental centers. Some models can be operated by one person, while others require two people.

Concrete footings hold deck posts in place and support the weight of the deck. Check local codes to determine the size and depth of footings required for your area. In cold climates, footings must be deeper than the soil frost line.

To help protect posts from water damage, each footing should be poured so that it is 2" above ground level. Tube-shaped forms let you extend the footings above ground level.

It is easy and inexpensive to mix your own concrete by combining portland cement, sand, gravel, and water. See pages 82 to 83 for more information on buying and mixing concrete.

Before digging, consult local utilities for location of any underground electrical, telephone, or water lines that might interfere with footings.

Everything You Need:

Tools (page 84): power auger or clamshell posthole digger, tape measure, pruning saw, shovel, reciprocating saw or handsaw, torpedo level, hoe, trowel, shovel, old toothbrush, plumb bob, utility knife.

Materials: 8" concrete tube forms, portland cement, sand, gravel, J-bolts.

Supplies: wheelbarrow, scrap 2 × 4.

How to Dig & Pour Post Footings

1 Dig holes for post footings with a clamshell digger or power auger, centering the holes on the layout stakes. For holes deeper than 35", use a power auger to dig post-hole footings.

2 Measure hole depth. Local building codes specify depth of footings. Cut away tree roots, if necessary, using a pruning saw.

3 Pour 2" to 3" of loose gravel in the bottom of each footing hole. Gravel will provide drainage under concrete footings.

4 Add 2" to hole depth so that footings will be above ground level. Cut concrete tube forms to length, using a reciprocating saw or handsaw. Make sure cut is straight.

5 Insert tubes into footing holes, leaving about 2" of tube above ground level. Use a level to make sure tops of tubes are level. Pack soil around tubes to hold them in place.

(continued next page)

6 Mix dry ingredients for concrete in a wheelbarrow, using a hoe.

7 Form a hollow in center of dry concrete mixture. Slowly pour a small amount of water into hollow, and blend in dry mixture with a hoe.

8 Add more water gradually, mixing thoroughly until concrete is firm enough to hold its shape when sliced with a trowel.

9 Pour concrete slowly into tube form, guiding concrete from wheelbarrow with a shovel. Use a long stick to tamp the concrete, filling any air gaps in the footing.

10 Level the concrete by pulling a 2 × 4 across the top of the tube form, using a sawing motion. Add concrete to any low spots. Retie the mason's strings on the batterboards, and recheck measurements.

11 Insert a J-bolt at an angle into the wet concrete at center of the footing.

12 Lower the J-bolt slowly into the concrete, wiggling it slightly to eliminate any air gaps.

13 Set the J-bolt so ¾" to 1" is exposed above concrete. Brush away any wet concrete on bolt threads with an old toothbrush.

14 Use a plumb bob to make sure the J-bolt is positioned exactly at center of post location.

15 Use a torpedo level to make sure the J-bolt is plumb. If necessary, adjust the bolt and re-pack concrete. Let concrete cure, then cut away exposed portion of tube with a utility knife.

Setting Posts

Posts support the deck beams and transfer the weight of the deck to the concrete footings. For maximum strength, the posts must be plumb.

To prevent rot or insect damage, use pressure-treated lumber for posts, and make sure the factory-treated end faces down.

Use metal post anchors to attach the posts to the concrete footings. Post anchors have drainage holes and pedestals that raise the ends of the wood posts above the concrete footings.

Everything You Need:

Tools (page 84): pencil, framing square, ratchet wrench, tape measure, power miter box or circular saw, hammer, screwgun, level, combination square.

Materials: metal post anchors, nuts for J-bolts, lumber for posts, 6d galvanized common nails, 2" wallboard screws.

Supplies: long, straight 2 × 4; 1 × 4s; pointed 2 × 2 stakes.

How to Attach Post Anchors

1 Mark the top of each footing as a reference line for installing post anchors. Lay a long, straight 2 × 4 flat across two or three concrete footings, parallel to the ledger, with one edge tight against the J-bolts.

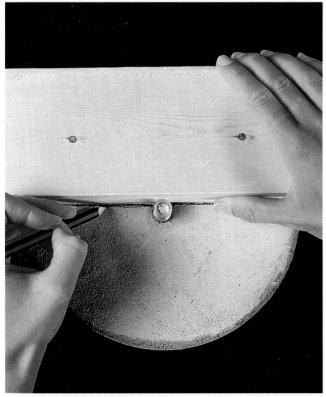

2 Draw a reference line across each concrete footing, using the edge of the 2 × 4 as a guide. Remove the 2 × 4.

3 Place a metal post anchor on each concrete footing, and center it over the J-bolt.

(continued next page)

How to Attach Post Anchors (continued)

4 Use a framing square to make sure the post anchor is positioned square to the reference line drawn on the footing.

5 Thread a nut over each J-bolt, and tighten it securely with a ratchet wrench.

How to Set Posts

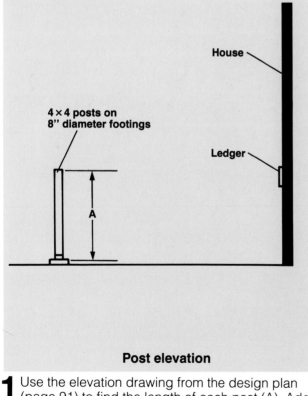

House

4 × 4 posts on 8" diameter footings

Ledger

A

Post elevation

1 Use the elevation drawing from the design plan (page 91) to find the length of each post (A). Add 6" for a cutting margin.

2 Cut posts with power miter box or circular saw. Make sure factory-treated ends of posts are square. If necessary, square them by trimming with a power miter box or circular saw.

3 Place post in anchor, and tack into place with a single 6d galvanized common nail.

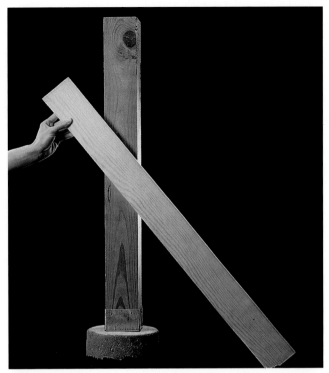

4 Brace post with a 1 × 4. Place the 1 × 4 flat across post, so that it crosses the post at a 45° angle about halfway up.

5 Attach the brace to the post temporarily with a single 2" wallboard screw.

6 Drive a pointed 2 × 2 stake into the ground next to the end of the brace.

(continued next page)

7 Use a level to make sure the post is plumb. Adjust the post, if necessary.

8 Attach the brace to the stake with two 2'' wallboard screws.

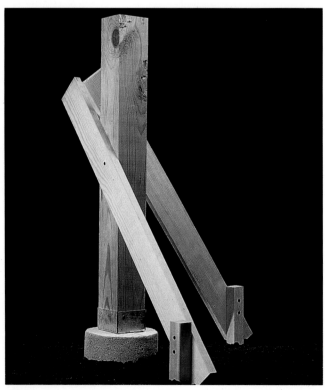

9 Plumb and brace the post on the side perpendicular to the first brace.

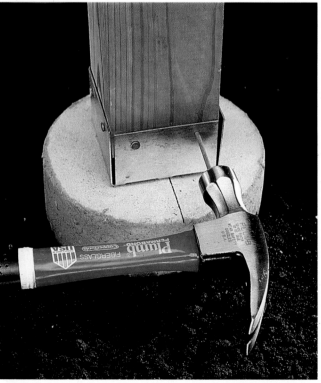

10 Attach the post to the post anchor with 6d galvanized common nails.

11 Position a straight 2 × 4 with one end on ledger and other end across face of post. Level the 2 × 4, then lower its post end ¼" for every 3 ft. between ledger and post (for water runoff). Draw a line on the post along the bottom of the 2 × 4. For cantilevered construction (pages 118 to 120), this line indicates the top of the joists. For corner-post construction (page 121), this line indicates the top of the beam.

12 For cantilevered construction, draw a line as shown in step 11. Then measure down a distance equal to width of joists, and mark the post.

13 Use a square to draw a line completely around the post. This line indicates the top of the canti-lever beam.

Installing a Beam & Hanging Joists

A deck beam is attached to the posts, and helps support the weight of the joists and decking. The method for installing the beam depends on whether the deck is a cantilevered or corner-post design.

A **cantilevered deck** has posts and one or more beams that are set back from the edge of the deck. The advantage is a neater and more attractive appearance. In cantilevered construction, the joists run across and extend past the beam. The general rule is the overhanging, or cantilevered, portion of the deck may be one-third the total length of the joists.

A **corner-post deck** has posts that are set at the edge of the deck. Because joists butt into the beam, rather than run across the top, corner-post construction is ideal for low decks.

Joists provide support for the decking boards. In cantilever construction, joists are attached to the ledger and header joist with galvanized metal joist hangers, and are nailed to the top of the beam. In corner-post construction, joists are attached to

the ledger and inside of the beam with galvanized joist hangers.

For strength and durability, use pressure-treated lumber for all beams and joists. The exposed outside joists and header joist can be faced with redwood or cedar boards for a more attractive appearance (page 129).

Everything You Need:

Tools (page 84): tape measure, pencil, hammer, circular saw, paint brush, combination square, screwgun, drill, twist bits (1/16", 1/8", 1/4"), 1" spade bit, ratchet wrench, caulk gun, reciprocating saw or handsaw.

Materials: pressure-treated lumber, clear sealer-preservative, 2½" corrosion-resistant deck screws, 3/8" × 4" lag screws and 1" washers, 3/8" × 5" lag screws (for corner-post deck), 10d galvanized common nails, 1¼" joist nails, joist angle brackets, galvanized metal joist hangers, silicone caulk.

How to Install a Beam for a Cantilevered Deck

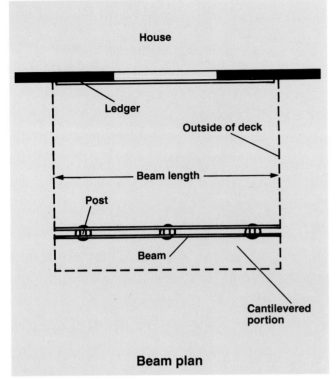

Beam plan

1 Use the deck design plan (page 90) to find the beam length. In plan shown above, the cantilever beam is cut to match overall width of deck.

2 Measure and mark two straight pressure-treated boards to length. Cut boards with a circular saw. Seal cut ends with clear sealer-preservative.

3 Hold beam boards together. Measure and mark the post locations on the tops and sides of boards, using a combination square as a guide.

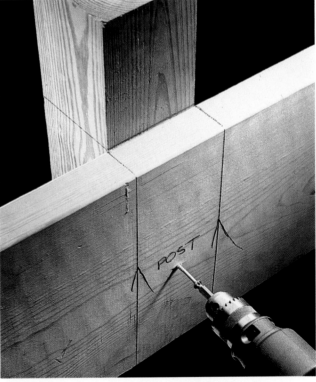

4 Position one beam board against the sides of the posts with crown side up. Marks on the board should be aligned with beam height marks on posts. Hold board in position with 2½" deck screws.

(continued next page)

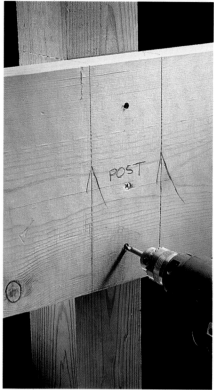

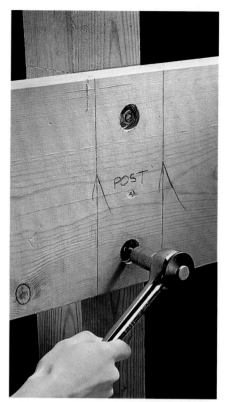

5 Drill two ¼'' pilot holes through the beam board and into each of the posts.

6 Counterbore each pilot hole to ½'' depth, using 1'' spade bit.

7 Attach board to posts with ⅜'' × 4'' lag screws and washers, using a ratchet wrench.

8 Attach the remaining beam board to the opposite sides of the posts, repeating steps 4 to 7. Seal screw heads with silicone caulk.

9 Cut tops of posts flush with top edge of beam, using a reciprocating saw or handsaw. Seal cut ends of posts with clear sealer-preservative.

How to Install a Beam for a Corner-post Deck

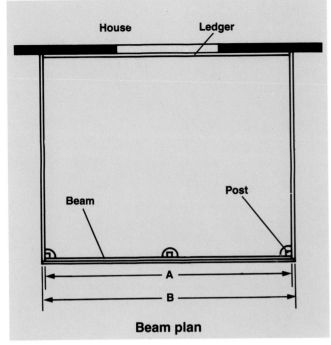

Beam plan

1 Use deck design plan (page 90) to find length of beam. Measure distance (A) between outside edges of corner posts. Mark pressure-treated board to length and cut with circular saw. Cut a second beam board (B), 3" longer than first board. Seal cut ends with clear sealer-preservative.

2 Position shorter beam board against outside of posts so that ends are flush with post edges. Top edge of board should be flush with beam height marks on posts. Drill ⅛" pilot holes, and hold beam board in position with 2½" deck screws.

3 Position the longer beam board against outside of the first board, so that ends overhang by 1½" to allow for outside joists. Fasten boards together with a pair of 2½" deck screws driven every 2 feet.

4 Drill two ¼" pilot holes through both beam boards and into each post. Counterbore each pilot hole to ½" depth, using a 1" spade bit. Secure boards to posts with ⅜" × 5" lag screws and washers, using a ratchet wrench. Seal screw heads and crack between boards with silicone caulk.

121

How to Hang Joists

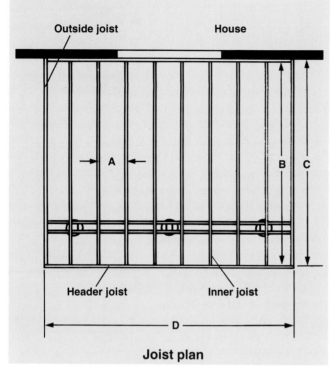

Joist plan

1 Use the design plan (page 90) to find the spacing (A) between joists, and the length of inner joists (B), outside joists (C), and header joist (D). Measure and mark lumber for outside joists, using a combination square as a guide. Cut joists with a circular saw. Seal cut ends with clear sealer-preservative.

2 Drill three 1/16" pilot holes, spaced about 3" apart, through one end of each outside joist.

3 Hold the outside joists in position at ends of ledger with 10d nails driven into the ledger.

4 Attach the outside joists to the top of the beam by toenailing them with 10d nails.

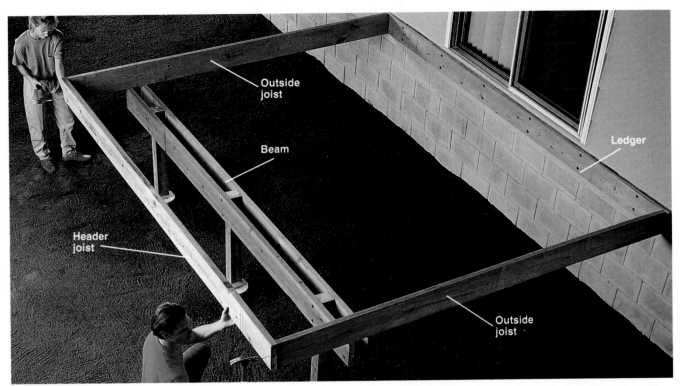

5 Measure and cut header joist. Seal cut ends with clear sealer-preservative. Drill 1/16" pilot holes at each end of header joist. Attach header to ends of outside joists with 10d galvanized nails.

6 Strengthen each inside corner of the deck frame with an angle bracket. Attach the brackets with 1¼" joist nails.

Alternate for corner-post deck: Position outside joist against post, flush with end of beam. Drill ¼" pilot holes through end of joist, into post. Counterbore pilot holes to depth of ½"; using 1" spade bit. Attach with ⅜" × 4" lag screws and washers. Cut off posts flush with top of beam, using a reciprocating saw or handsaw.

(continued next page)

7 Measure along ledger from edge of outside joist, and mark where joists will be attached to ledger.

8 Draw the outline of each joist on the ledger, using a combination square as a guide.

9 Measure along the beam from outside joist, and mark where joists will cross beam. Draw the outlines across top of both beam boards.

10 Measure along the header joist from the outside joist, and mark where joists will be attached to header joist. Draw the outlines on the inside of the header, using a combination square as a guide.

11 Attach joist hangers to the ledger and to the header joist. Position each hanger so that one of the flanges is against the joist outline. Nail flange to framing member with 1¼" joist nails.

12 Cut a scrap board to use as a spacer. Hold spacer inside each joist hanger, then close the hanger around the spacer.

13 Nail the remaining side flange to the framing member with 1¼" joist nails. Remove spacer.

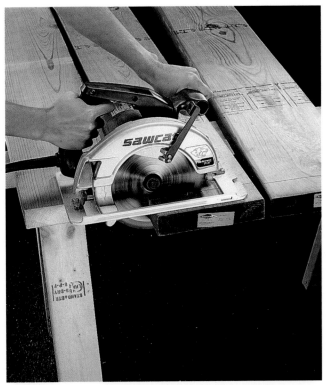

14 Measure and mark lumber for joists, using a combination square as a guide. Cut joists with a circular saw.

(continued next page)

How to Hang Joists (continued)

15 Seal cut ends with clear sealer-preservative. Place joists in hangers with crowned side up.

16 Attach the ledger joist hangers to the joists with 1¼" joist nails. Drive nails into both sides of each joist.

17 Align the joists with the outlines drawn on the top of the beam. Anchor the joists to the beam by toe-nailing from both sides with 10d galvanized nails.

18 Attach the joists to the header joist hangers with 1¼" joist nails. Drive nails into both sides of each joist.

Laying Decking

Buy decking boards that are long enough to span the width of the deck, if possible. If boards must be butted end-to-end, make sure to stagger the joints so they do not overlap from row to row. Predrill the ends of boards to prevent screws or nails from splitting the wood.

Install decking so that there is a ⅛" gap between the boards to provide drainage. If you install the ledger using standoff brackets (see page 96), install the first row of decking in step 1 flush with the backside of the ledger, leaving the gap between the house and ledger uncovered. Boards naturally "cup" as they age. Lay boards with the bark side facing down, so that the cupped surface cannot hold standing water.

Everything You Need:

Tools (page 84): tape measure, circular saw, screwgun, hammer, drill, ⅛" twist bit, pry bar, chalk line, jig saw or handsaw.

Materials: decking boards, 2½" corrosion-resistant deck screws, galvanized common nails (8d, 10d), redwood or cedar facing boards.

How to Lay Decking

1 Position the first row of decking flush against the house. First decking board should be perfectly straight, and should be precut to proper length. Attach the first decking board by driving a pair of 2½" corrosion-resistant deck screws into each joist.

2 Position remaining decking boards so that ends overhang outside joists. Space boards about ⅛" apart. Attach boards to each joist with a pair of 2½' deck screws driven into each joist.

Alternate method: Attach decking boards with 10d galvanized common nails. Angle the nails toward each other to improve holding power.

(continued next page)

3 If boards are bowed, use a pry bar to lever them into position while fastening.

4 Drill ⅛" pilot holes in ends of boards before attaching them to outside joists. Pilot holes prevent screws from splitting decking boards at ends.

5 After every few rows of decking are installed, measure from edge of the decking board to edge of header joist. If measurements show that the last board will not fit flush against the edge of the deck, adjust board spacing.

6 Adjust board spacing by changing the gaps between boards by a small amount over three or four rows of boards. Very small spacing changes will not be obvious to the eye.

7 Use a chalk line to mark the edge of decking flush with the outside edge of deck. Cut off decking with a circular saw. Set saw blade ⅛" deeper than thickness of decking so that saw will not cut side of deck. At areas where circular saw cannot reach, finish cutoff with a jig saw or handsaw.

8 For a more attractive appearance, face the deck with redwood or cedar facing boards. Miter-cut corners, and attach boards with deck screws or 8d galvanized nails.

Alternate facing technique: Attach facing boards so that edges of decking overhang facing.

Building Stairs

Building deck stairs requires four calculations.

Number of steps depends on the vertical drop of the deck. The vertical drop is the distance from the surface of the deck to the ground.

Rise is the vertical space between treads. Building codes require that the rise measurement be about 7".

Run is the depth of the treads. A convenient way to build deck stairs is to use a pair of 2×6s for each tread.

Span is figured by multiplying the run by the number of treads. The span lets you locate the end of the stairway, and position support posts.

Everything You Need:

Tools (page 84): tape measure, pencil, framing square, level, plumb bob, posthole digger, wheelbarrow, hoe, circular saw, hammer, drill, ⅛" twist bit, 1" spade bit, ratchet wrench, caulk gun.

Materials: sand, portland cement, gravel, J-bolts, metal post anchors, 2×12 lumber, metal cleats, ¼" $\times$ 1¼" lag screws, joist angle brackets, 1¼" galvanized joist nails, ⅜" $\times$ 4" lag screws and 1" washers, 2×6 lumber, 16d nails, silicone caulk.

Supplies: long, straight 2×4; pointed stakes; masking tape.

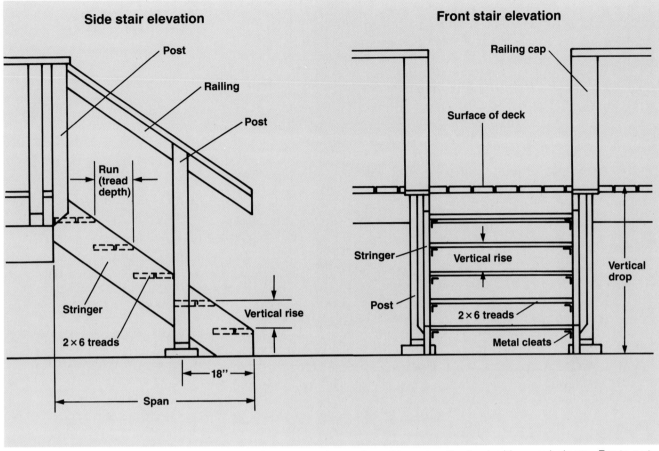

Side stair elevation

Post

Railing

Post

Run (tread depth)

Stringer

2 × 6 treads

Vertical rise

18"

Span

Front stair elevation

Railing cap

Surface of deck

Stringer

Vertical rise

Post

2 × 6 treads

Metal cleats

Vertical drop

A deck stairway is made from two 2 × 12 stringers, and a series of treads attached with metal cleats. Posts set 18" back from the end of the stairway help to anchor the stringers and the railings. Calculations needed to build stairs include the **number of steps**, the **rise** of each step, the **run** of each step, and the stairway **span**.

How to Find Measurements for Stairway Layout

Sample Measurements (39" High Deck)

1. Find the number of steps: Measure vertical drop from deck surface to ground. Divide by 7. Round off to nearest whole number.	Vertical drop:			39"
	÷ 7 =			5.57"
	Number of steps:	=	=	6
2. Find step rise: Divide the vertical drop by the number of steps.	Vertical drop:			39"
	Number of steps:	÷	÷	6
	Rise:	=	=	6.5"
3. Find step run: Typical treads made from two 2 × 6s have a run of 11¼". If your design is different, find run by measuring depth of tread, including any space between boards.	Run:			11¼"
4. Find stairway span: Multiply the run by the number of treads. (Number of treads is always one less than number of steps.)	Run:			11¼"
	Number of treads:	×	×	5
	Span:	=	=	56¼"

How to Build Deck Stairs

1 Use the stairway elevation drawings (page 131) to find measurements for stair stringers and posts. Use a pencil and framing square to outline where stair stringers will be attached to the side of the deck.

2 Locate the post footings so they are 18" back from the end of stairway span. Lay a straight 2 × 4 on the deck so that it is level and square to side of deck. Use a plumb bob to mark the ground at centerpoints of footings.

3 Dig holes and pour footings for posts (pages 108 to 111). Attach metal post anchors to footings and install 4 × 4 posts (pages 112 to 117).

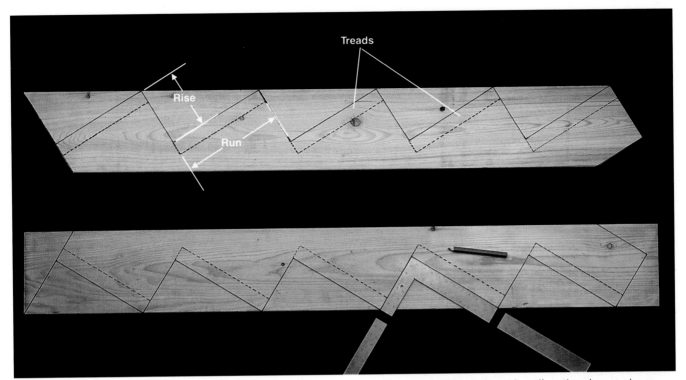

Treads

Rise

Run

4 Lay out stair stringers. Use tape to mark the rise measurement on one leg of a framing square, and the run measurement on the other leg. Beginning at one end of stringer, position the square with tape marks flush to edge of board, and outline the rise and run for each step. Then draw in the tread outline against the bottom of each run line. Use a circular saw to trim ends of stringers as shown.

5 Attach metal tread cleats flush with bottom of each tread outline, using 1/4" × 1 1/4" lag screws. Drill 1/8" pilot holes to prevent the screws from splitting the wood.

6 Attach angle brackets to upper ends of stringers, using 1 1/4" joist nails. Brackets should be flush with cut ends of stringers.

(continued next page)

7 Position the stair stringers against side of deck, over the stringer outlines. Align top point of stringer flush with the surface of the deck. Attach stringers by nailing the angle brackets to the deck with 1¼" joist nails.

8 Drill two ¼" pilot holes through each stringer and into each adjacent post. Counterbore each hole to depth of ½", using a 1" spade bit. Attach stringers to posts with ⅜" × 4" lag screws and washers, using a ratchet wrench. Seal screw heads with silicone caulk.

9 Measure width of stair treads. Cut two 2 × 6s for each tread, using a circular saw.

10 For each step, position the front 2 × 6 on the tread cleat, so that the front edge is flush with the tread outline on the stringers.

11 Drill ⅛" pilot holes, then attach the front 2 × 6s to the cleats with ¼" × 1¼" lag screws.

12 Position the rear 2 × 6s on the cleats, allowing a small space between boards. Use a 16d nail as a spacing guide. Drill ⅛" pilot holes, and attach 2 × 6s to cleats with ¼" × 1¼" lag screws.

Stair Variations

Hardware option: Metal step brackets can be attached to tops of stringers. This method allows the treads to overhang at the sides.

Notched stringers made of pressure-treated wood are available precut at building centers. Edges of cut-out areas should be coated with sealer-preservative to prevent rot.

Installing a Deck Railing

Railings must be sturdy, and should be firmly attached to the framing members of the deck. Never attach railing posts to the surface decking. Check local building codes for guidelines regarding railing construction. Most codes require that railings be at least 34" above decking, vertical balusters should be spaced less than 4" apart, and fully graspable handrails should attach to stairway railings (check local codes before purchasing handrail material to ensure that it meets code requirements.)

Everything You Need:

Tools (page 84): tape measure, pencil, power miter box, drill, ¼" twist bits (⅛", ¼"), 1" spade bit, combination square, awl, ratchet wrench, caulk gun, level, reciprocating saw or circular saw, jig saw with wood-cutting blade.

Materials: railing lumber (4 × 4s, 2 × 6s, 2 × 4s, 2 × 2s), clear sealer-preservative, ⅜" × 4" lag screws and 1" washers, silicone caulk, 2½" corrosion-resistant deck screws, 10d galvanized common nails.

How to Install a Deck Railing

Railing detail

1 Refer to the deck design plan (pages 90 to 91) for spacing (A) and length of railing posts and balusters. Posts should be spaced no more than 6 feet apart.

2 Measure and cut 4 × 4 posts, using a power miter box or circular saw. Cut off tops of the posts square, and cut the bottoms at 45° angle. Seal cut ends of lumber with clear sealer-preservative.

3 Measure and cut balusters for main deck, using a power miter box or circular saw. Cut off tops of the balusters square, and cut bottoms at 45° angle. Seal cut ends of lumber with clear sealer-preservative.

4 Drill two ¼'' pilot holes through bottom end of each post, spaced 4'' apart. Counterbore each pilot hole to ½'' depth, using a 1'' spade bit.

5 Drill two ⅛'' pilot holes near bottom end of each baluster, spaced 4'' apart. Drill two ⅛'' pilot holes at top of each baluster, spaced 1½'' apart.

(continued next page)

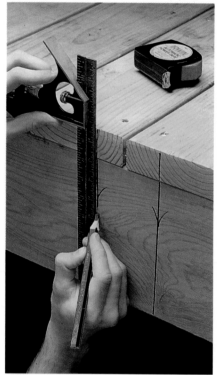  

6 Measure and mark position of posts around the outside of the deck, using a combination square as a guide. Plan to install a post on outside edge of each stair stringer.

7 Position each post with beveled end flush with bottom of deck. Plumb post with a level. Insert a screwdriver or nail into pilot holes and mark side of deck.

8 Remove post and drill ¼" pilot holes into side of deck.

9 Attach railing posts to side of deck with ⅜" × 4" lag screws and washers, using a ratchet wrench. Seal screw heads with silicone caulk.

10 Measure and cut 2 × 4 side rails. Position rails with edges flush to tops of posts, and attach to posts with 2½" corrosion-resistant deck screws.

11 Join 2 × 4s for long rails by cutting ends at 45° angle. Drill 1/16" pilot holes to prevent nails from splitting end grain, and attach rails with 10d galvanized nails. (Screws may split mitered ends.)

12 Attach ends of rails to stairway posts, flush with edges of posts, as shown. Drill 1/8" pilot holes, and attach rails with 2½" deck screws.

13 At stairway, measure from surface of decking to the top of the upper stairway post (A).

14 Transfer measurement A to lower stairway post, measuring from the edge of the stair stringer.

(continued next page)

15 Position 2 × 4 rail against inside of stairway posts. Align rail with top rear corner of top post, and with the pencil mark on the lower post. Have a helper attach rail temporarily with 2½" deck screws.

16 Mark the outline of the post and the deck rail on the back side of the stairway rail.

17 Mark the outline of the stairway rail on the lower stairway post.

18 Use a level to mark a plumb cutoff line at the bottom end of the stairway rail. Remove the rail.

19 Extend the pencil lines across both sides of the stairway post, using a combination square as a guide.

20 Cut off lower stairway post along diagonal cutoff line, using a reciprocating saw or circular saw.

21 Use a jig saw to cut the stairway rail along the marked outlines.

22 Position the stairway rail flush against top edge of posts. Drill 1/8" pilot holes, then attach rail to posts with 2 1/2" deck screws.

(continued next page)

23 Use a spacer block to ensure equal spacing between balusters. Beginning next to a plumb railing post, position each baluster tight against spacer block, with top of baluster flush to top of rail. Attach each baluster with 2½" deck screws.

24 For stairway, position baluster against stringer and rail, and adjust for plumb. Draw diagonal cutoff line on top of baluster, using top of stair rail as a guide. Cut baluster on marked line, using power miter box. Seal ends with clear sealer-preservative.

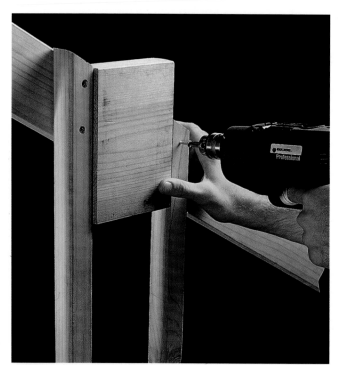

25 Beginning next to upper stairway post, position each baluster tight against spacer block, with top flush to top of stair rail. Attach baluster with 2½" deck screws.

26 Position 2 × 6 cap so edge is flush with inside edge of rail. Drill ⅛" pilot holes, and attach cap to rail with 2½" deck screws driven every 12". Also drive screws into each post and into every third baluster. For long caps, bevel ends at 45°. Drill ¹⁄₁₆" pilot holes, and attach at post using 10d nails.

27 At corners, miter ends of railing cap at 45°. Drill ⅛" pilot holes, and attach cap to post with 2½" deck screws.

28 At top of stairs, cut cap so that it is flush with stairway rail. Drill ⅛" pilot holes and attach cap with 2½" deck screws.

29 Measure and cut cap for stairway rail. Mark outline of post on side of cap. and bevel-cut the ends of the cap.

30 Position cap over the stairway rail and balusters so that edge of cap is flush with inside edge of rail. Drill ⅛" pilot holes, and attach cap to rail with 2½" deck screws driven every 12". Also drive screws through cap into stair post and into every third baluster. Attach a fully graspable handrail to the rail.

Finishing a New Deck

Finish a deck with clear sealer-preservative or staining sealer. Sealer-preservatives protect wood from water and rot, and are often used on cedar or redwood, because they preserve the original color of the wood. If you want the wood to look weathered, wait several months before applying sealer-preservative.

Staining sealers, sometimes called toners, are often applied to pressure-treated lumber to give it the look of redwood or cedar. Staining sealers are available in a variety of colors.

For best protection, use finishing products with an alkyd base. Apply fresh finish each year.

Everything You Need:

Tools: orbital sander, sandpaper, shop vacuum, pressure sprayer, eye protection, paint brush.

Materials: clear sealer-preservative or staining sealer.

Use an orbital sander to smooth out any rough areas before applying finish to decking boards, railings, or stair treads.

How to Finish a Redwood or Cedar Deck

1 Test wood surface by sprinkling water on it. If wood absorbs water quickly, it is ready to be sealed. If wood does not absorb water, let it dry for several weeks before sealing.

2 Sand rough areas and vacuum deck. Apply clear sealer to all wood surfaces, using a pressure sprayer. If possible, apply sealer to underside of decking and to joists, beams, and posts.

3 Use a paint brush to work sealer into cracks and narrow areas that could trap water.

How to Finish a Pressure-treated Deck

1 Sand rough areas and vacuum the deck. Apply a staining sealer (toner) to all deck wood, using a pressure sprayer.

2 Use a paint brush to smooth out drips and runs. Porous wood may require a second coat of staining sealer for even coverage.

Platform Deck

A platform deck is built low to the ground, so it is ideal for a flat, level yard, and when the height of the interior floor is close to the surface of the yard.

Because it is low to the ground, a platform deck does not require railings or stairs. It has an open, airy feeling that makes it an ideal place for sunning or entertaining.

The platform deck shown at left adds visual interest with a second level and redwood decking laid on the diagonal. The decking is a mix of cream-colored sapwood, and reddish heartwood that is rot-resistant. Always treat sapwood with a clear sealer-preservative.

A redwood facing board runs around the edges of this deck. Redwood that comes in contact with the ground or with grass should be treated with a clear sealer-preservative before installation.

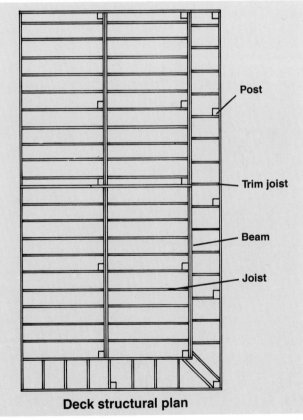

Deck structural plan

Low platform deck uses 2 × 6 joists and corner-post beams that require closely spaced posts for extra support. Joists for interior portion of deck are spaced 12" on-center to support longer spans of diagonal decking. Short joists (called trim joists) around the perimeter of the deck support the border decking boards.

How to Build a Platform Deck

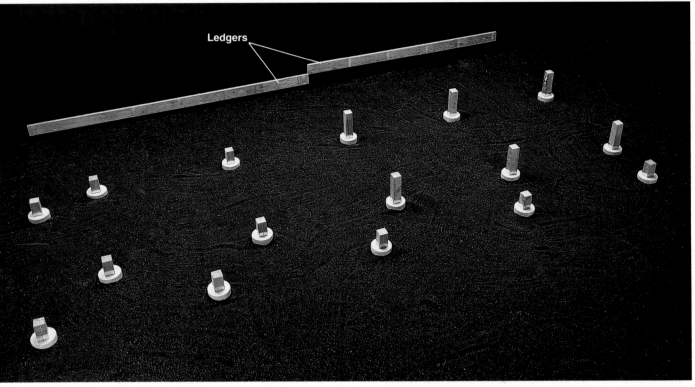

Ledgers

1 Attach 2 × 6 pressure-treated ledgers to house with ³⁄₈" × 4" lag screws (pages 96 to 101). Pour footings and install 4 × 4 pressure-treated posts (pages 108 to 117). Mark posts to indicate tops of beams.

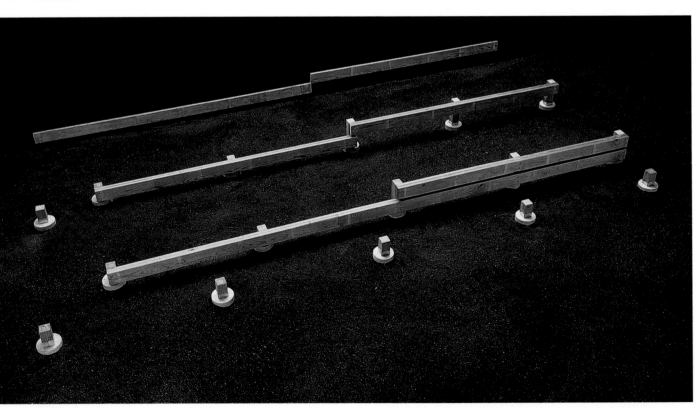

2 Build each beam from a pair of pressure-treated 2 × 6s (pages 118 to 121). Hold 2 × 6s together with 2½" corrosion-resistant deck screws driven every 18". Drill counterbored pilot holes and attach beams to posts with ³⁄₈" × 5" lag screws. Cut all post tops flush with tops of beams.

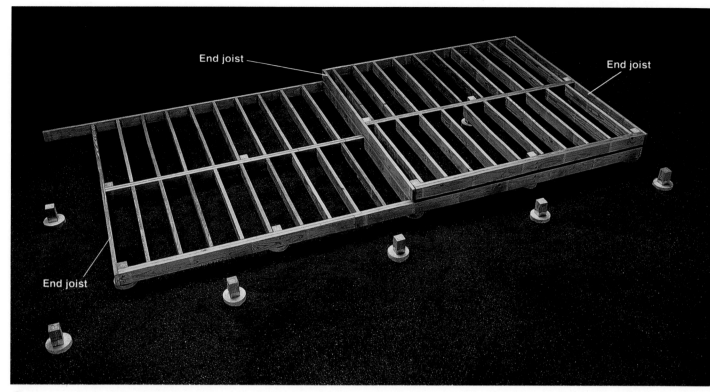

3 Hang pressure-treated joists (pages 122 to 126). Lay out interior joists at 12" on-center. Install all joists with galvanized joist hangers and joist nails. Attach end joists to posts, not beams, with 2½" deck screws. End grain has little holding power.

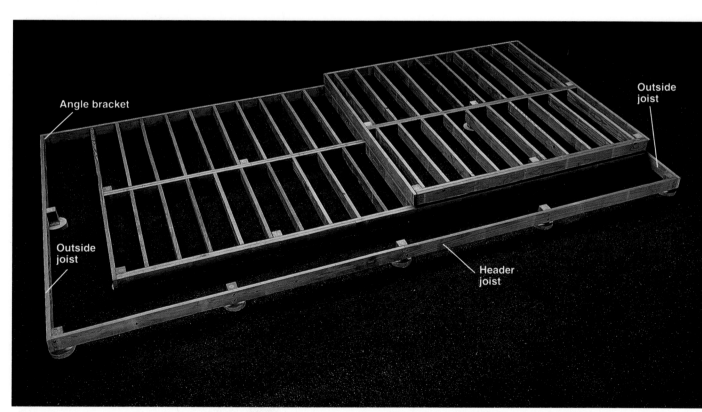

4 Attach 2 × 6 pressure-treated outside joists and header joist to posts, using ⅜" × 3" lag screws (pages 122 to 123). Counterbore pilot holes so that facing boards can be installed. Reinforce inside corners of outside joists with angle brackets. Cut off all post tops flush with tops of header and outside joists.

(continued next page)

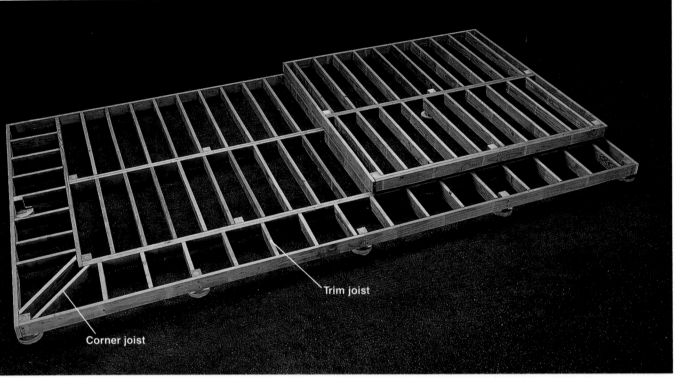

Trim joist

Corner joist

5 Lay out trim joists at 16" on-center. Attach the trim joists with galvanized joist hangers and joist nails. Cut the ends of the diagonal corner joists at a 45° angle, and install with angled joist hangers.

6 Install all diagonal decking (pages 127 to 129). Decking boards that will butt against the house should be pre-mitered at 45°. Use a chalk line to snap a cutoff line across the overhanging decking, flush with outside edges of beams and end joists. Cut off decking with circular saw with blade depth set to match thickness of decking.

Herringbone pattern

7 Install the decking border. Begin with board against diagonal pattern, and work toward outside edge of deck. Adjust spacing between decking so that the edge of the last board is exactly flush with edge of header or outside joist (page 128). Stagger the ends of the boards at corner to create a herringbone pattern, as shown.

Facing boards

8 Install facing boards (page 129). Top edge of facing should be flush with top of decking. For appearance, choose top-grade lumber for facing. Miter the corners at 45°, and fasten facing boards with 2½" corrosion-resistant deck screws driven every 18".

Diamond-pattern Deck

Give your deck a distinct look with an unusual decking pattern. The visual appeal of a deck can be improved by using a diagonal or diamond-shaped decking pattern, like the one at left.

Install double joists or a row of double blocking for extra strength and stability wherever ends of decking boards butt together. Space the joists at 12" on-center to support the diagonal decking.

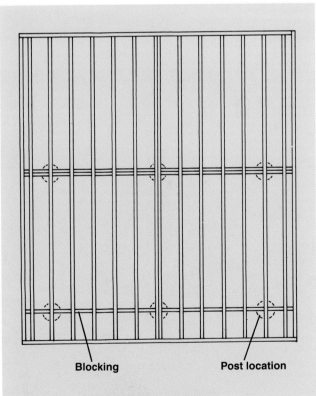

Blocking   **Post location**

Deck structural plan

Diamond-pattern deck has blocking added to provide surface for attaching ends of decking. Joist spacing on diagonal decking pattern is 12" on-center.

How to Build a Diamond-pattern Deck

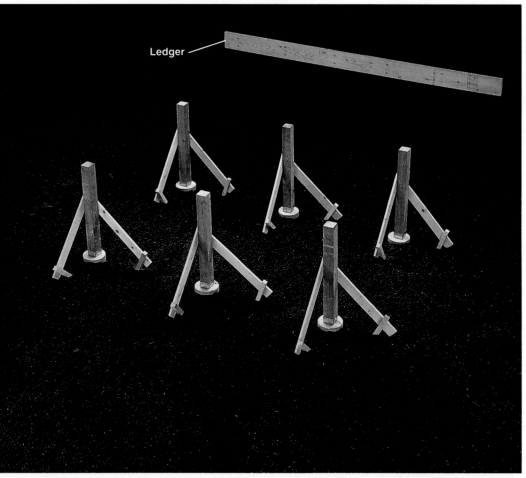

Ledger

1 Install pressure-treated ledger (pages 96 to 101).

Pour post footings and install 4 × 4 pressure-treated posts (pages 108 to 117). Seal all cut ends of lumber with sealer-preservative.

Brace all posts longer than 2 feet (pages 115 to 116).

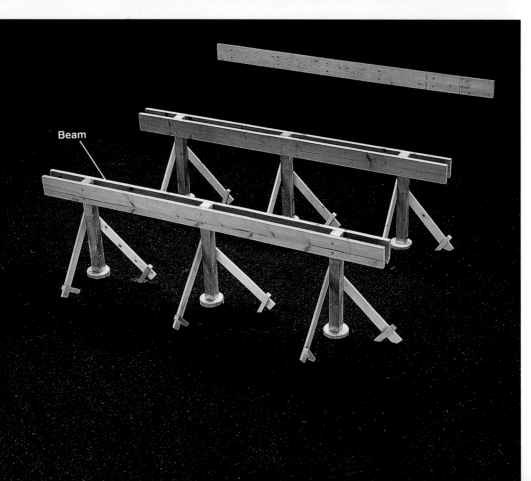

Beam

2 Build each deck beam from pressure-treated lumber (pages 118 to 121). Position the boards against the row of posts, and drill a pair of ¼" pilot holes through boards and into each post. Attach the beam to the posts with ⅜" × 4" galvanized lag screws and washers.

Cut off all post tops flush with the top edges of the beams, using a reciprocating saw or handsaw.

3 Cut the header and outside joists from pressure-treated lumber.

Attach the outside joists to the ledger and to the tops of the beams, using 10d galvanized nails.

Attach the header joist to the ends of the outside joists, using 10d nails, then reinforce inside corners with angle brackets (page 123).

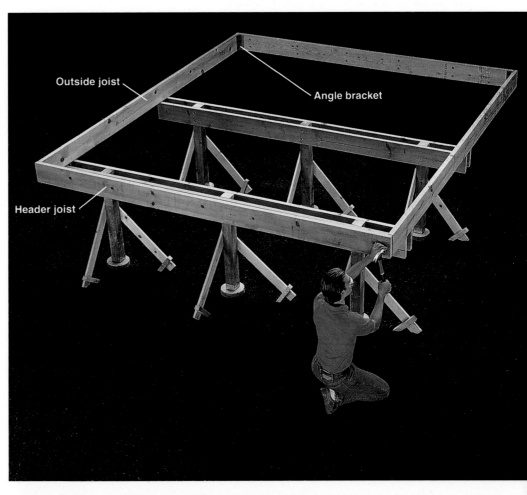

Outside joist

Angle bracket

Header joist

4 Hang the inside joists (pages 122 to 126).

Attach the joists to the ledger and header joist with galvanized metal joist hangers.

Install a double joist at the center of the framework to provide extra support where the ends of the decking boards will butt together.

Toenail all joists to the tops of the beams with 10d galvanized nails. Seal seam between double joists with silicone caulk.

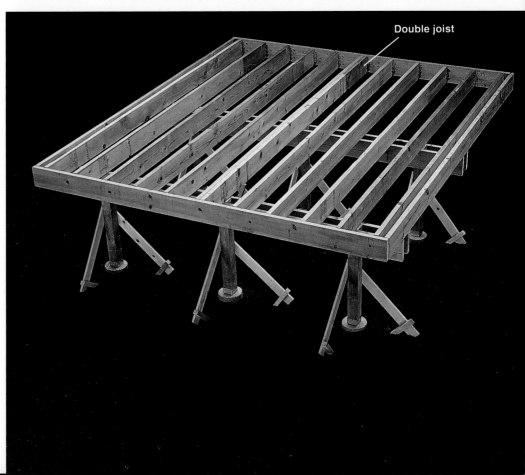

Double joist

(continued next page)

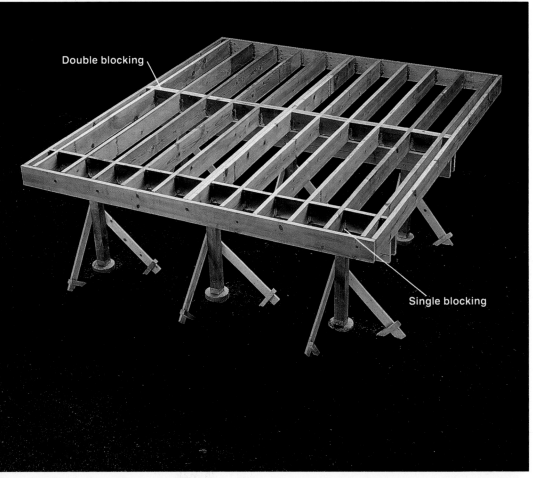

Double blocking

Single blocking

5 Install a row of double blocking between each pair of joists at the center of the diamond pattern, using galvanized joist hangers.

Install a row of single blocking at the end of the diamond pattern joist, using galvanized joist hangers. Blocking provides support where the ends of the diagonal decking boards form a continuous line.

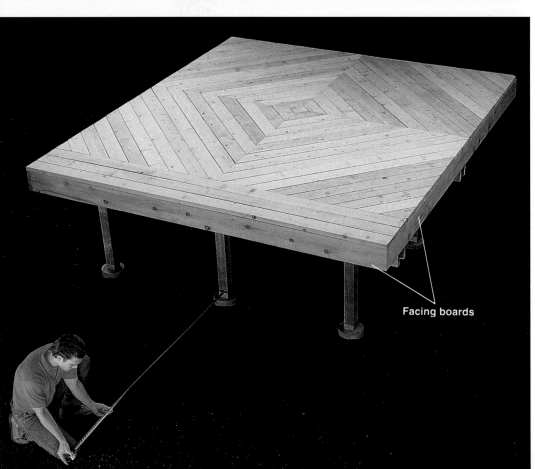

Facing boards

6 Face the header and outside joists with high-quality boards (page 129). Miter the corners of the boards at 45°, and attach with 8d galvanized nails.

Lay 2 × 6 redwood decking (pages 127 to 129). Use a combination square to mark the ends of angled boards at 45°, and cut with a circular saw or a power miter box.

Lay out the deck stairs (pages 130 to 131).

7 Pour stairway footings, and install post anchors and 4 × 4 posts.

Build the deck stairs (pages 130 to 135). The 2 × 10 stringers are attached to side of deck with ⅜" × 4" lag screws driven through back of header joist, and are anchored to the stairway posts with ⅜" × 4" lag screws.

Attach the stair treads to the stringers with metal cleats and lag screws.

8 Build post-and-baluster railing for the deck and stairway (pages 136 to 143).

Attach the 4 × 4 posts to the deck with ⅜" × 6" lag screws. Attach the 2 × 4 horizontal rails, the rail cap, and 2 × 2 balusters with 2½" corrostion-resistant deck screws. Attach a fully graspable handrail. For a decorative detail, let posts and balusters extend below facing boards.

Index